The Last Years of the
Somerset
& Dorset

The Last Years of the
Somerset
& Dorset

Colin G. Maggs

BLP

Contents

First published 1991
by Ian Allan Ltd
This impression 1997

ISBN 1 901945 04 9

Published by Book Law Publications and printed by Ian Allan Printing Ltd at its works at Coombelands in Runnymede, England.

Half title:
'7F' No 53806 blasts its way up the 1 in 50 out of Bath with the 11am freight to Evercreech in July 1962. *C. P. Walker*

Title page:
Ivatt 2MT No 41243 arrives at Midford with the 6.05pm Bath-Binegar local on 11 August 1961. *The Late Derek Cross*

Introduction 5

1 Outline history 6

2 Description of the line:

Bath to Bournemouth 15

Highbridge branch 48

Wells branch 57

Bridgwater branch 60

3 Railwaymen's reminiscences 64

4 Run down and closure 77

5 Locomotive allocations 128

Acknowledgements
Grateful acknowledgement for assistance is due to Christopher Steane without whose photographs and notes this book could never have been written; to Norman Slipp and George A. A. Tucker for checking the manuscript and to numerous Somerset & Dorset men for providing reminiscences. I should like to acknowledge the photographic expertise of Cynthia Bradford of Oxford, who made the majority of the black and white prints used in this book.

Introduction

The Somerset & Dorset Joint Railway (S&D) has always been a railway to bring out emotions in people. In the past it may have aroused feelings of fury as passengers waited at Templecombe or Evercreech Junction for poorly timed connections. For its employees the line was small enough for everyone to know everyone else, which gave the feeling of a big happy family (or usually so); with everyone working for the good of each other. The S&D was not merely lines, earthworks and buildings, it was people and a way of life. Today, although the track has been lifted and many of its buildings demolished, quite a significant number who love the line remain – some former employees, others part of a large band of enthusiasts.

Today the latter look back with nostalgia, and wonder at the thought that London, Midland & Scottish Railway (LMS) engines actually travelled to the south coast. In the latter years of the S&D there was a great deal of anticipation over what would head an expected train. Would it be ex-LMS, a BR Standard, or ex-Southern Railway locomotive, or perhaps one built by the Great Western Railway (GWR)?

And would a passenger train be headed by a passenger locomotive? The S&D was not averse to using goods locomotives on passenger trains. The most unusual example, though relatively common on summer Saturdays, was the unique Class 7F 2-8-0s built specially for hauling heavy goods and mineral trains over the Mendips, and certainly not designed for mixed-traffic work. Or the passenger train might be in the charge of an 0-6-0 or BR Standard Class 9F 2-10-0, mixed-traffic engines yes, but with a leaning towards freight working rather than passenger, yet on the S&D such engines could be seen on passenger workings almost every day.

Rolling stock was even more varied. Ex-LMS coaches were common and much of the ex-SR stock was still in malachite green rather than BR maroon. Even a rake of ex-London & North Eastern Railway coaches appeared on the Cleethorpes to Exmouth train on Saturdays, while ex-GWR coaches were also to be seen.

This wide variety of locomotives and rolling stock amidst the green rolling downlands of southern England, downlands which presented fearsome gradients for trains to tackle, expresses often having to be double-headed. In the 1950s there could be seen the contrast of a new BR Standard locomotive, or an almost new SR air-smoothed Pacific piloted by a 40-year-old Midland 4-4-0. Furthermore, the S&D right up until closure had unique features that were not part of the Western Region, or the Southern Region, but were peculiar to the S&D itself, the passenger and freight headcodes being just one example.

Then there was the longevity of the S&D. Very much threatened with closure after the withdrawal of through trains in September 1962, the dreaded event seemed to be staved off by reprieve after reprieve and led one to believe that a line with such a character and of quite respectable length was really immortal, and would indeed go on for ever. Even when the last trains ran on 6 March 1966, one could not really believe that the end had come and that we would wake up the next day and find the timetable worked as usual.

1
Outline history

The Somerset & Dorset Joint Railway has a complicated history — complicated because it was not built as a whole, but was many parts joined together like a construction kit. Basically it consisted of a union between the Somerset Central Railway (SCR) and the Dorset Central Railway (DCR).

The SCR was initiated by James Clark, a skin dresser and sheepskin rug manufacturer of Street who, as an entrepreneur, wished to improve communications in order to expand his business. Present at the first meeting were two directors of the Bristol & Exeter Railway (B&E), eager to be associated with what it hoped would be an expansion of its territory. Although the Glastonbury Canal, opened in 1833, connected the port of Highbridge with Glastonbury on the Somerset wetlands, this was hardly the latest thing in transport, so a group of like-minded men proposed the SCR. This opened in 1854

linking Highbridge Wharf with Glastonbury, the line being laid economically either along, or close to, the bank of the erstwhile canal. Being associated with the B&E the track was laid to the broad gauge and, as was usual with most small railways, worked by a larger company, in this case the B&E.

A businessman never rests content, and no sooner had the line been completed when it was realised that it was not really complete and needed extending at both ends. Burnham was reached in 1858 and Wells the following year. Burnham gave the company access across the Bristol Channel to South Wales, principally for the carriage of passengers who would otherwise have had to travel round via Gloucester, the Severn Tunnel not being opened until 1 December 1886.

The S&D had shipping interests at Highbridge Wharf for freight, and Burnham

Right:
Opening of the Somerset Central Railway: procession in the grounds of the ruined Glastonbury Abbey, 17 August 1854. Either Somerset country bumpkins or *Illustrated London News* engravers spelt 'There's' incorrectly.
Courtesy Illustrated London News

Top right:
Floods at Glastonbury & Street around the turn of the century.
Colin G. Maggs Collection

Bottom right:
Boiler shop, Highbridge c1900.
Colin G. Maggs Collection

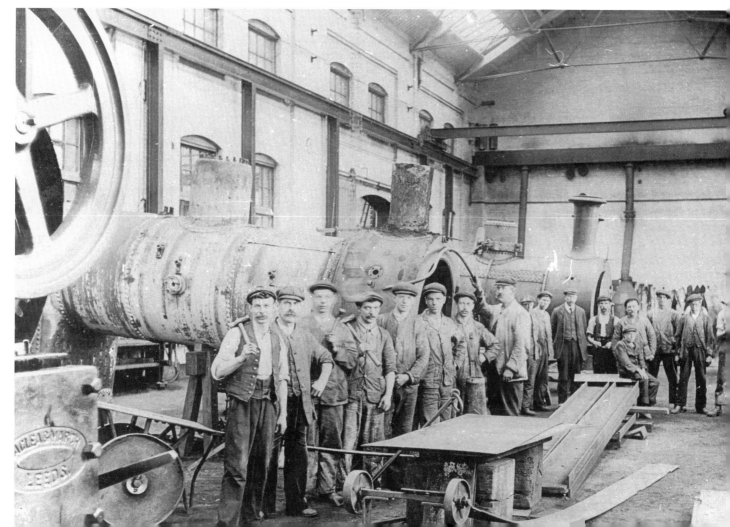

for passengers; although the Cardiff passenger ferry ceased in 1888, the LMS took over the cargo ships and ran them until 1934. The S&D had its own steam cranes at Highbridge Wharf and also at its jetty at Bridgwater. Highbridge Wharf continued to be used by vessels until about 1950.

The extension to Wells opened up traffic to and from the ecclesiastical centre of the area, the SCR being the first line to reach the city. The East Somerset and the Cheddar Valley lines not arriving until 1862

and 1870 respectively. Yet despite these extensions the SCR still remained a fairly minor rural line; though the directors realised that it was trunk routes which paid the best dividends.

To the south lay the DCR, interestingly enough the remains of a much more ambitious project, the South Midland Union Railway (SMUR) which was to have run from the Midland Railway (MR) at Mangotsfield (the MR's branch to Bath was not then built) and to have followed approxi-

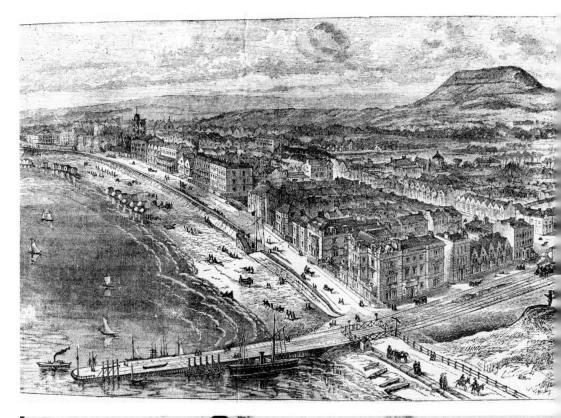

Above right:
Burnham: S&D train shed lower right; pier for railway-owned cross-Channel packets, centre. The level crossing with gates across both road and rail is interesting. It is not known whether it is depicted accurately by the artist. The hill in the background is Brent Knoll, 457ft above sea level.
Colin G. Maggs Collection

Right:
S&D 0-4-4T No 12 with roofless cab at Evercreech Junction shortly after the locomotive was built in 1877.
Colin G. Maggs Collection

mately the course of the later S&D to Poole. The SMUR planned as a standard gauge line was naturally opposed by the GWR and its broad gauge associates, as well as the Dorset landowners.

In 1855 a much curtailed version was proposed — the DCR — a standard gauge line to run from Wimborne, only five miles inland from Poole, as far as Blandford.

The project persuaded the SCR to make yet another extension, this time from Glastonbury to Bruton, ostensibly to link with the broad gauge Wilts, Somerset & Weymouth Railway (WSWR) and thus have its proposal supported by the GWR and associates, but with the real intention of joining the DCR. Curiously enough the DCR's Act of Parliament received Royal Assent on exactly the same day as that of the SCR's Bruton extension. There was a further coincidence in that the authorised capital of the DCR and the SCR's extension were identical.

The DCR then planned an extension from Blandford to meet the SCR at Bruton. No attempt was made to conceal this aim, it being openly stated that it was 'not only to accommodate the traffic of the district, but by means of other lines to complete a continuous line of about 70 miles in length, from the English Channel at Poole and Southampton to the Bristol Channel at Highbridge'.

In 1859 the SCR obtained powers to add standard gauge rails to its line, though at this juncture it had not been decided whether to lay the standard gauge in addition to, or instead of, broad gauge rails. The following year the decision was in favour of the latter, complete conversion costing £80,000 less than mixed gauge. The B&E, it will be remembered, provided the locomotives and rolling stock to run the S&D, so was naturally angered by its partner's decision and sought to force its hand by ending the working agreement.

Repercussions were expected in the 1861 Session of Parliament. The SCR was putting forward its Bill for the abandonment of broad gauge on the Bruton extension and sought more time for the completion of the line. The SCR did not escape from the battle scot-free. It was compelled to concede that the Bruton extension 'should be provided with rails for both gauges' and the B&E forced the building of the broad gauge connection with the WSWR which the SCR wished to abandon now it was consorting with the Dorset Central. This spur was never used and its earthworks can still be seen today just north of Cole where the SCR crossed what is now the main line to the West of England.

The SCR had a big problem. It had undertaken to work the DCR from Templecombe to Bruton as soon as this line was completed and furthermore also had to find locomotives, rolling stock and labour to operate its own lines when the agreement with the B&E terminated in 1861. In the event the agreement expired and the DCR's Templecombe to Bruton extension was ready for opening before the SCR had the necessary equipment. Fortunately the B&E made a magnanimous gesture and allowed the SCR to hire broad gauge stock until it was in a position to take over working on the standard gauge. Although the DCR extension to Bruton (this station was later renamed Cole) was ready in November 1861, it was not opened until February 1862, on the same date as the Glastonbury to Cole extension. From this day the SCR worked its own line on the standard gauge.

The SCR and DCR were amalgamated the following August to form the Somerset & Dorset Railway, the new company taking for its seal a design including on the left a train passing Glastonbury Abbey and Glastonbury Tor, and on the right the Arms of Dorchester. The S&D was extended from Templecombe to Blandford in 1863 and by means of running powers over the LSWR to Poole, the S&D could now finally operate between the English and Bristol Channels. Quite an achievement, but to what purpose? There cannot have been all that number of persons wishing to travel from Poole to Burnham and Cardiff, or from Cardiff to Poole and although gallant attempts were made to make the S&D part of a through route to Paris by running a ferry service between Poole and Cherbourg, this particular shipping venture had to be abandoned due to losses in 1865 and 1866.

The S&D was now in a very poor financial state and its only hope of success was a daring plan: an extension from Evercreech over the Mendip Hills to Bath where it was to connect with the MR. Such a line opened up exciting possibilities. In addition to tapping colliery traffic from the Radstock coalfield and quarry traffic from the Mendips, it was anticipated that the line would become an important through route between north and south and not be a mere rural railway.

This extension was opened in 1874 and from this date the Bath to Bournemouth section became the main line, with the Burnham to Evercreech Junction section being relegated to secondary status. Unfortunately the bold addition of the Bath Extension did not quite succeed as insufficient capital was available to work it efficiently — rolling stock was inadequate; there were not enough sidings or crossing

Diagrammatic map showing opening and closing dates.

N

R. SEVERN

Severn Tunnel

Gloucester

MANGOTSFIELD

BRISTOL

Opened 4.8.1869
Closed 7.3.66p 31.5.71g

Swindon

Bath Jn

BATH

YATTON

Devonshire Tun.

Combe Down Tunnel

Newbury / Reading

Midford

TROWBRIDGE

Wellow

Shoscombe & Single Hill Halt

Taunton

Midsomer Norton & Welton

RADSTOCK

Reading

BATH-EVERCREECH JN
Opened 20.7.1874

Chilcompton

WESTBURY

Burnham on Sea

Binegar

Summit 811ft

FROME

Wharf

HIGHBRIDGE

Opened 3.5.1858
Closed 8.9.62p 20.5.63g

Bason Bridge

Màsbury Halt

HIGHBRIDGE-
GLASTONBURY
Opened 28.8.1854

WELLS

Winsor Hill Tunnels

Opened 15.3.1859
Closed 29.10.51

Polsham

SHEPTON MALLET

Edington Jn

West Pennard

Shapwick

Cossington

Ashcott

GLASTONBURY

Pylle

Evercreech New

BATH – BLANDFORD
Closed
7.3.66

Bawdrip Halt

EVERCREECH JN

Wharf

BRIDGWATER

BASON BRIDGE-EVERCREECH JN
Closed 7.3.66

Cole for Bruton

BRIDGWATER-
EDINGTON JN.
Opened 21.7.1890
Closed 1.12.52p
1.10.54g

Taunton

WINCANTON

GLASTONBURY – TEMPLECOMBE
Opened 3.2.1862

Salisbury

TEMPLECOMBE

Henstridge

Stalbridge

TEMPLECOMBE – BLANDFORD
Opened 31.8.1863

Exeter

Sturminster Newton

Shillingstone

Stourpaine & Durweston

BLANDFORD – WIMBORNE
Opened 1.11.1860

Note :– HIGHBRIDGE – BASON BRIDGE Closed 2.10.72

BLANDFORD

Closed 11.7.20g
17.6.33p

Charlton Marshall Halt

Spetisbury Halt

Brockenhurst

SOMERSET & DORSET JOINT RLY

G.W.R

BLANDFORD – BROADSTONE
Closed 7.3.66p
6.1.69g

Bailey Gate

Corfe Mullen SB

WIMBORNE

L.M.S (M.R)

Corfe Mullen Halt

Opened 14.12.1885

S.R (L.S.W.R)

Broadstone Jn

POOLE

Parkstone

Branksome

B'MOUTH CENTRAL

p = passenger   g = goods

BOURNEMOUTH WEST

Scale   0   4   8   12   16   Miles

Weymouth

10

loops and manpower was deficient, both numerically and in the necessary skills of running a railway. If only a relatively little more finance had been available it would have been a success, but alas no more cash could be raised and the only real solution was to sell.

Despite the fact that the S&D was linked to the standard gauge MR at its northern end and the standard gauge London & South Western Railway (LSWR) at its southern end, the S&D approached the Great Western with a view of selling, perhaps reasoning that the GWR would offer a magnificent sum to prevent the S&D being snapped up by its enemies, the MR and the LSWR. However, the GWR did not

leap at the chance of purchasing the S&D, but consulted with the B&E. Time seemed no object and three months after the initial approach, the two broad gauge companies decided to bring in the LSWR with a view to its taking over the S&D south of Templecombe. The LSWR was surprised to hear of the line being up for sale and lost no time in taking positive action. Archibald Scott, the LSWR general manager, immediately met James Allport, his Midland counterpart. They inspected both the line and its books; reported to their respective directors who then made a much better offer for the S&D than had been made by the GWR and the B&E — and all this within a week. Terms of the lease to the standard gauge companies

was sufficient to allow the S&D to pay 3½% interest on the Bath Extension ordinary stock as well as on all the debenture dividends which it had been unable to do before. The Somerset & Dorset Joint Railway as it had become on being taken over by the MR and LSWR, adopted a crest combining the Arms of Bath and the seal of Dorchester.

The S&D was run by a Joint Committee whose policy was consolidation rather than expansion. Considerable effort was put into doubling the track, installing Tyer's electric tablet, providing adequate locomotives and rolling stock, training staff, attracting and developing traffic both local and through. Bath and Templecombe both saw a great increase in exchange traffic, especially in the

TUESDAY, Sept. 1st to 4th, the Band of the

ESSEX REGIMENT

S. & D.J.R.

EXCURSIONS FROM BATH (L.M. & S. STATION).

EVERY WEEK DAY.—Cheap Tickets to Burnham-on-Sea and Wells at 6.45, 8.30, and 11.20 a.m., and every week day. Cheap Day Tickets to Radstock and Midsomer Norton by any ordinary train.

EVERY WEDNESDAY, THURSDAY AND SATURDAY, Excursion Tickets to the Mendip Hills, including Chilcompton (for Downside Abbey), Masbury (for Wells), etc., at 8.30, 11.20 a.m. 1.25 p.m. and 2.50 p.m. as specified on bills.

FRIDAYS, for 8 or 15 days, to various places in the South of England, at 3.50 p.m. and to the West of England, North and South Devon and Cornwall at 11.20 a.m. and 3.50 p.m. as specified on bills, and for 8 or 15 days to Bridgwater, Highbridge and Burnham-on-Sea at 11.20 a.m.

SATURDAYS.—Day Trip to Bournemouth at 7.50 p.m.

WEEK-END TICKETS to all parts.

GEO. H. WHEELER, traffic Supt.

Left:
S&D advertisement in the *Bath Chronicle* 29 August 1925.
Colin G. Maggs Collection

Facing page, top:
'Small' S&D 4-4-0 No 14 leaving Bath for Bournemouth West. The bonded store can be seen above the roof of the first coach, an LMS vehicle. Note the two loading gauges on the left — the S&D being the lower.
Real Photographs

Facing page, bottom:
A busy scene at Templecombe No 2 Junction c1929. On the right an 0-4-4T heads a train to Evercreech Junction; a 'Large' 4-4-0 stands on the incline up to the station while a Fowler 0-6-0T waits on the single track to Templecombe Lower. The engine shed can be seen in the distance on the far left. A fine gas lamp stands outside No 2 signalbox from which this photograph was taken.
Colin G. Maggs Collection

staple commodities of coal, stone and milk, all this leading to the doubling of net receipts between 1876 and 1881. Many private sidings were opened, especially during the early years of the Joint Committee, serving such industries as brick and tile, bakery, fuller's earth, collieries, quarries, wagon works, sawmills, timber merchants, brewery, dairy and peat workings.

To have to travel either north or south via Wimborne was frustrating as it involved a reversal and the loss of time uncoupling the locomotive and running round the train. This irritation was avoided by building a three-mile long cut-off from Corfe Mullen to Broadstone.

The only expansionist line built by the SDJR was the Bridgewater (sic) Railway Co which opened a branch from Edington in 1890. In all but name it was part of the SDJR bringing the length of the system up to 102 miles.

Both world wars brought even more traffic to the well-used line. Troop and supply trains were worked southwards and hospital trains northwards; ammunition and weapons were carried including tanks. During World War 1 the Admiralty opened a pumping station at Corfe Mullen, the S&D laying a siding to bring in fuel. At Milldown, north of Blandford, a siding was opened to serve a German prisoner-of-war camp, while to the south of the town a three-mile long railway was built to a military camp.

It was a similar story during World War 2 with war supplies and personnel moving south and hospital trains moving north. The line proved particularly vital in the weeks leading up to the Normandy landings on D-day. The former works area at Highbridge became a transit camp for United States Army troops, while War Department sidings were built high on the Mendips at Masbury.

Meanwhile the 1923 Grouping had taken place with very little immediate effect apart from the Bridgewater Railway being absorbed into the Southern Railway, though the S&DJR Co was itself dissolved and the SR and LMS became owners, rather than lessees. In due course operating economies were made, the chief of which was the closure of Highbridge Works in 1930, putting over 300 men out of work. The same year separate management of traffic was discontinued, the S&D being worked by the LMS leaving the SR responsible for civil engineering. The S&D locomotives were absorbed into LMS stock, a logical move as many of them were of LMS type. The coaches were taken over by the SR. In the early 1930s further economies were made: the two cargo vessels sold, the Wimborne line closed and Templecombe Lower put in

the charge of the Templecombe SR stationmaster. It was not all contraction in the first six years of Grouping, halts to combat bus competition were opened at Bawdrip, Charlton Marshall, Corfe Mullen, Shoscombe & Single Hill and Stourpaine & Durweston.

Fortunately in the 1930s bridges on the Mangotsfield to Bath line had been strengthened. This allowed Stanier Class 5 4-6-0s to work through and these were a great help hauling the summer Friday night/Saturday morning trains over the S&D from Bath to Bournemouth, the number of which had grown during that decade with the general introduction of a summer holiday for the masses. It was fortunate that many holidaymakers were willing to travel overnight and thus enjoy a full Saturday at the seaside, so that engines which had hauled Down trains were available at a fairly early hour on Saturday morning to take returning holidaymakers northwards.

Following Nationalisation things went on much as before, the line being worked by ex-LMS locomotives and commercially supervised by the Southern Region in which it was placed, the joint nature thus continuing.

When the regional boundaries were redrawn in the 1950s things became even more of a joint style. The Western Region took over commercial responsibility north of Cole; the Southern Region retained its hold to the south, while the London Midland Region loaned locomotive stock to the SR to operate the whole of the S&D. 1958 saw further regional changes when the WR assumed responsibility for the section from Bath to Henstridge and took charge of the locomotives and sheds at Bath, Radstock, Templecombe and Highbridge. In 1963 regional boundaries were redrawn yet again, with the WR taking over as far south as Shillingstone and also, incidentally, the former Southern main line from Salisbury to Exeter.

Just as Grouping led to certain economies and abandonments, so did Nationalisation. There were closures: Templecombe Lower Yard in 1950; the Wells branch and Highbridge to Burnham in 1951, though interestingly excursion trains continued to work through to Burnham for another 11 years; the Bridgwater branch closed in 1952. These were all relatively minor lines and few could criticise their passing. However, the real threat of total S&D closure came in 1962 when, at the end of the summer timetable, all through trains were withdrawn. The clock had now been turned back a century. Local traffic was insufficient to make the line economic and in 1966 most of the S&D was closed.

2
Description of the line:

Although technically Bath Green Park station was not S&D property, being only half a mile from the start of S&D metals it certainly warrants a description. Bath Green Park is a gem of a station, fortunately preserved and now restored to its former glory. It was opened in 1869 by the MR on the then outskirts of the city. Although Bradshaw's Railway Guide referred to it as 'Queen Square', this was a quite unofficial title and local people always called it the 'Midland station'. It only received the 'Green Park' suffix in 1951. The pseudo-Georgian front block in Bath stone with its imposing classical façade, slender Ionic columns above the rusticated ground floor, balustraded parapet and finely proportioned fenestration continues to be a joy to behold, admirably complementing the iron and glass train shed beyond which covers the plat-forms for about half their length. J. S. Crossley was the architect responsible for the train shed and J. H. Sanders for the façade.

Designed to avoid conflicting movements of passengers, the front of the building had a cast iron cab shelter to protect intending passengers from the elements. Within, they bought their tickets at small round-headed booking office windows where the clerk disappeared from view to find and date them. A large enamel departure indicator in the booking hall and platform finger post gave information which in later days was supplemented by a loudspeaker system.

There were two platform roads and two central sidings: one used for storing coaches, and the other as a run-round loop for releasing locomotives from incoming trains. The platform on the southern side held nine

Below:
Bath Green Park was the northern terminus of the S&D. It shared its facilities with the Midland line from Gloucester, Mangotsfield and Bristol. Constructed of Bath stone in 1869, it has an imposing classical façade, Ionic columns, triangular pediments to the flanking windows and a balustrade neatly concealing the roof line. In front a cast iron cab shelter protected intending passengers from the rain.
C. Steane

TELEGRAMS & ENQUIRIES
PARCELS AND
LEFT LUGGAGE
OFFICE
TURN LEFT.

bogie coaches and that on the northern, eight. Originally the northern platform was intended for arrivals having a carriage exit along that side of the station so passengers could conveniently step from train to road vehicle but for much of the station's existence, the platforms were interchangeable. Through expresses to and from the S&D normally used the southern platform as it was the longer, local trains using the north side. The platforms were short for an important station, but the cost of extending them across the river would have been prohibitive. On a long train, to avoid passengers to Bath being overcarried, the guard was required to pass through the rear vehicles which would have stopped off the end of the platform and request any passengers getting out to proceed along the corridor to a coach nearer the front. LMS guards working passenger trains destined for the S&D were required, on arrival at Bath, to hand over to the guard working forward the numbers and description of vehicles and the train's tonnage; S&D guards were given similar instuctions. At Bath, two Midland carriage and wagon examiners checked all S&D rolling stock before it went over the

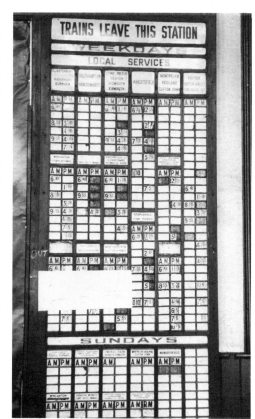

Facing page:
Inside the spacious booking hall, barriers steered one passenger at a time towards the booking office or enquiry window. Until closure the station was lit by gas. *C. Steane*

Left:
The attractive enamel train indicator which faced passengers as they entered the booking hall. When photographed it had not been updated and had an 'Out of Order' label pasted over it. *C. Steane*

Below:
A platform indicator at the edge of the concourse directed passengers to their train. S&D services normally used the southern platform. In the last months of service the other terminus was Bournemouth Central, Bournemouth West being closed in August 1965. The word 'West' on the board is covered. *C. Steane*

17

MR, while two S&D men checked all Midland stock before it travelled over the S&D.

One unusual feature of the station was a bonded warehouse at the west end of the north platform. Vehicles containing wines and spirits consigned to local traders were shunted into this secure building, the casks were lowered to cellars extending the full length of the station platforms, storage being assisted by a hand-worked narrow gauge railway. In 1938 the area of the station in the region of the buffer stops was maintained by builder W. Mannings as an ornamental garden free of charge as an advertisement for his business.

Across the river from the station was the stone-built MR engine shed and the larger S&D one of timber construction. Originally a two-road shed, S&D traffic increased to such an extent that it became quite inadequate to handle the number of locomotives, and an almost identical shed was built immediately to the south. In 1883-84 the shed frontage was equalised by the earlier shed being lengthened by about 100ft and the second by 56ft. The S&D

depot was not much above river level and at times became flooded. The rising gradient of about 1 in 40 from the shed to the main line led to wheel slip, particularly when a dead engine was being hauled out. Although the first S&D Class 7F 2-8-0 had been built in 1914, 20 years later it was still not possible to turn this type at Bath because the turntable was too short. In 1935 a 60ft diameter table was installed. A new brick-built coaling stage in 1954 replaced the old one of timber construction.

On the opposite side of the line was the large stone-built MR goods shed and coal sidings, while further west, on the north side, was Bath gas works and Bath Junction yard. Trains from the Midlands arrived on No 1 road; roads 2 and 3 were used to form trains for Templecombe and Bournemouth, while No 4 road was for Bath transfers. No 5 road held 'short traffic', that is, wagons which were going only a few miles down the S&D and could be taken on the 5.50am all-stations to Templecombe rather than be conveyed by a through train.

Bath Junction signalbox stood in the fork where the S&D line diverged from that to

Above:
View across the Avon to the rear of the stone-built former MR locomotive shed. Beyond the stone base of the water tower is the rear of the S&D timber-built engine shed. Wagons stand on the 'Boat Road', so called because it gave access to a quay where traffic was transferred between rail and MR barges. MR barges worked along the Kennet & Avon Canal to Trowbridge.
C. Steane

Left:
Class 9F 2-10-0 No 92243 stands dead beside the MR shed, 'Steam for ever' chalked on its smokebox. To the right of the signal can be seen the stone-built Bonded Store. Spirits were unloaded in here and stored in cellars beneath the platform.
C. Steane

Mangotsfield. One economy made after Grouping was, in 1924, the replacement of the LMS Bath Junction signalbox and the nearby S&D's Bath Single Line Junction signalbox by a new Bath Junction signalbox. A few yards beyond, the lines converged to become the single track section to Midford; this never being doubled because of the expense of widening or duplicating Devonshire and Combe Down Tunnels.

The electric train tablet was automatically picked up from the lineside apparatus by the jaws of the catcher attached to most locomotives working over the S&D. This apparatus was patented by the S&D's Locomotive Superintendent, Alfred Whit-

aker. The tablet was contained in a neat leather pouch like a Lilliputian mailbag with a looped handle which claws on the engine, or a lineside post, grabbed at the beginning and end of each single line section. As distances were quite critical and a swaying tender could cause the apparatus to miss, a driver always had his hand ready to apply the brake so that if a malfunction occurred he could stop and let his fireman run back to collect the tablet. In the event of an engine not being fitted with the exchange apparatus, a pouch with a large hoop was used for hand exchange.

Freight trains over a certain weight were banked up the gradient of 1 in 50 to Combe

Left:
S&D Class 7F 2-8-0 No 53806 climbs the 1 in 50 gradient out of Bath with the 2.00pm freight to Evercreech Junction on 27 April 1962. Most of the wagons are empties bound for local collieries. The engine carries the S&D freight headcode. No 53806 is assisted by a banker whose exhaust can be seen below that of the '7F'. A siding to the Victoria Brick Works was formerly on the left. For many years the S&D line marked the limit of the built-up area of Oldfield Park. *Colin P. Walker*

Below:
Gradient profile of the S&D main line.

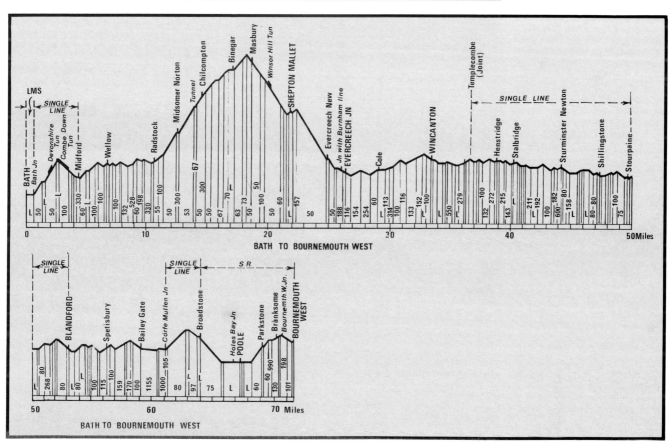

BATH TO BOURNEMOUTH WEST

BATH TO BOURNEMOUTH WEST

Down Tunnel and, in order to protect the banker, a special 'Bath Bank Engine Staff' was issued at Bath Junction box. The line curved and crossed over the GWR and then could be seen a brick works siding on the right and the Co-op siding further on to the left. The line climbed through the 447yd long Devonshire Tunnel with Lyncombe Vale beyond, the banker dropping off just before the entrance to the 1,829yd Combe Down Tunnel, the longest single bore without any ventilation shaft in the country. The guard of a loose-coupled freight train counted 10 rail beats and then applied his brake for he knew then that the descent at 1 in 100 had started.

A walker on the footpath near the Midford end of the tunnel could smell the dank and smoky atmosphere being blown

out, especially if there was a north-westerly wind. Immediately before the 95yd long brick-built Tucking Mill Viaduct the cutting was unusually wide to allow for Combe Down station to be erected. It never was — not surprising as people would not have wanted to climb 350ft to Combe Down laden with shopping.

Because Midford station was built in an awkward situation on the ledge of a hillside, it had two goods yards, one north and one south of the station. Latterly Midford signalbox differed from the others on the Bath Extension because the original was largely destroyed by a runaway train on 29 July 1936 causing the Southern Railway to provide a 'temporary replacement' with a flat roof; this replacement surviving until the line's closure 30 years later! The box worked

Left:
The sylvan approach to Combe Down Tunnel from the north and only a mile as the crow flies from the city centre. *C. Steane*

Left:
View from the north portal of Combe Down Tunnel showing its horseshoe shape section. A permanent way hut stands on the left. *C. Steane*

Below:
Class 8F 2-8-0 No 48444 and brake van emerging from the south portal of Combe Down Tunnel. It is proceeding from Bath to Writhlington to collect loaded coal wagons on an afternoon in February 1966. The arched stone pitching to the right of the locomotive supports the cutting. The striped box at the foot of the post to the right of the engine contains a telephone in case a locomotive should stall and the driver needs to communicate with the Midford signalman. The cutting and public footpath to the left always smelled dank caused by the air coming from the tunnel. *C. Steane*

Above:
Midford station in 1961: Class 2 2-6-2T No 41243 shedded at 82C Bath Green Park, has brought the 6.05pm Bath to Binegar local through the single line section on 11 August. The metal lattice mast supported a cut out metal semaphore resembling an X laid on its side. This was to control movements in the 'wrong' direction. At the station the railway runs on a ledge, roofs of houses can be seen below to the right of the locomotive's buffer.
The Late Derek Cross

Right:
The Midford signalman has a friendly word with the footplate crew of an '8F' 2-8-0 proceeding with brake van to pick up wagons at Writhlington.
C. Steane

a relatively rare signal. Shaped like an 'X' on its side, it was known as a 'wrong road' signal which could authorise a train to be signalled from the single line back to the Up line of double track. This feature was necessary when an Up train stalled between Midford and the tunnel. Using a lineside telephone, a driver could advise the Midford signalman of the problem. He would then send a 'blocking back' bell code to the Wellow box and on receiving acknowledgement, would instruct the driver to back down to Midford and would pull off both 'wrong road' signals which authorised the driver to pass the Down home signals at danger.

On the far side of the 168yd long Midford Viaduct, the line was doubled. This viaduct crossed the Somerset Coal Canal and the GWR's Limpley Stoke to Hallatrow branch; the latter famous for being the location of the Ealing comedy film 'The Titfield Thunderbolt'.

The line between Midford and Radstock was particularly sinuous due to following the

bed of the Somerset Coal Canal which wended its way along the valley of the Wellow Brook, keeping to the north side and turning with the hills' spurs and re-entrants. In places the canal was too sinuous even for the S&D, and loops of the former canal bed can still be seen untouched by the S&D's formation.

Wellow was the first station on the line south of Bath built to the standard Bath Extension design with a bay-windowed stationmaster's office, a combined booking hall and waiting room and a ladies' room.

Shoscombe & Single Hill halt, built in concrete sections from the SR's concrete depot at Exmouth Junction, was opened by

Above:
Midford Viaduct from above: an S&D Class 7F 2-8-0 No 53809 pilots 'West Country' 4-6-2 No 34103 *Calstock* on the 12.20pm Saturdays-only Bournemouth West to Nottingham on 1 September 1962. *B. J. Ashworth*

Left:
Class 8F 2-8-0 No 48706 shunting coal wagons at Writhlington Colliery in the afternoon of a day in February 1966. Slag heaps can be seen both sides of the line. Movements are controlled by Writhlington signalbox almost hidden by smoke. *C. Steane*

Right:
The loading plant at Writhlington Colliery. Loaded wagons run by gravity to make room for empties. Narrow gauge 'tubs' are stored on the right. Writhlington signalbox can be seen in the background on the left. *C. Steane*

George Lansbury MP. The halt was well used as buses could not reach the area due to narrow lanes, and to reach a bus route would have involved the inhabitants in a 1½-mile long climb uphill.

Beyond the 53yd long Home Farm Viaduct was Writhlington Colliery and as it remained open after the closure of most of the S&D, was latterly served by trains from the ex-GWR Radstock line. The coal was loaded by chutes into standard gauge BR steel wagons which were shunted out on to the colliery sidings. During the last few

months of the S&D, each afternoon an engine came out from Bath to collect loaded wagons, Class 8F 2-8-0 No 48706 frequently being employed.

Coal from Tyning Colliery was taken across the S&D to the GWR and the very low Tyning Bridge (popularly known as 'Marble Arch') which formerly spanned the Somerset Coal Canal tramway, prevented the use of standard height locomotives and, from 1929, Sentinel geared 0-4-0 shunters Nos 47190 and 47191 were used until their withdrawal in 1961 and 1959 respectively.

Above:
Ex-S&D 0-4-0 Sentinel No 47191 outside Radstock shed, 14 August 1959. *Colin G. Maggs*

Left:
This weird Heath-Robinson device for coaling engines stood in the yard at Radstock. It swivelled on a pivot, and lifted small tubs with wheels, one tub helping to counterbalance the other. *C. Steane*

27

Above:
Class 2P 4-4-0 No 40696 approaches Radstock North with the 1.10pm Bath to Templecombe on 23 August 1958. In the background are colliery tips and Radstock North 'A' signalbox which controlled entry to the engine shed and goods yard on the south side of the running lines. Note the telephone terminals on the signal post. *J. C. Beckett*

Right:
BR Standard Class 4MT 2-6-4T No 80146 stands at Radstock North with the emergency 14.00 service from Templecombe to Bath Green Park. The signal post has two arms so that despite the footbridge blocking the view, one or the other can be seen. The can on the platform has been brought from Writhlington signalbox to be refilled with drinking water. *C. Steane*

28

Approaching Radstock station, on the left was the two-road stone-built engine shed, erected c1890 by the Joint Committee to stable banking engines required to assist trains to Masbury, and also to house the local shunters. In later years the shed had three or four Class 3F 0-6-0Ts and two Sentinels. After closure in 1966 the shed was used by the Somerset & Dorset Railway Trust for some years before the group moved to Washford on the West Somerset Railway.

The level crossing on the Bath to Shepton Mallet road caused traffic hold-ups particularly on peak summer Saturdays, and the problem was compounded by the fact that even if the S&D gates were open to road traffic, the GWR level crossing gates just beyond might be closed. As far back as 1875 the Board of Trade had ordered a bridge to be built and, two years later, said it was about to take legal proceedings; but nothing

was ever done and the gates continued to hold up traffic until the last train ran from Writhlington on 16 November 1973. Writhlington, one of the last two pits in the area, had closed two months previously. On closure of the S&D, a link was opened south of Radstock station between the ex-GWR's Bristol & North Somerset line and the S&D in order to give access.

From Radstock the S&D climbed on a ruling gradient of 1 in 50 for 7½ miles to a summit at Masbury. It crossed the Bristol & North Somerset Railway by the 128yd long North Somerset Viaduct locally known as the 'Five Arches'. Just before Midsomer Norton station was Norton Hill colliery with its own National Coal Board shunting engine, while Midsomer Norton station itself had prize-winning flower beds and lawns. Beyond the twin-bore 64yd long Chilcompton Tunnel the line climbed to Chilcompton station. At Moorewood were

Above:
S&D Class 7F 2-8-0 No 53807 enters Radstock North with the 7.00am train from Templecombe to Bath on 15 August 1959. It was unusual to see an engine of this class on a stopping passenger train. When seen on passenger duties they usually headed a through train to or from the North rather than a local. A porter waits with sacks on a barrow. A subway is under the first coach for those in a hurry.
F. J. Saunders

29

Above:
BR Standard Class 4MT 2-6-0 No 76026 leaves Radstock across the 128yd long North Somerset Viaduct, unofficially known as the 'Five Arches', with the 06.45 Bath to Templecombe on the last day of regular passenger trains, 5 March 1966.   *P. Riley*

Right:
A BR Standard Class 4MT 2-6-4T crosses the GWR's North Somerset branch at 'Five Arches'. Radstock West's fixed caution board is prominent, left. The track bed of the Somerset Coal Canal's tramway from collieries at Welton is to the right of the North Somerset line.
C. Steane

Below right:
Chilcompton Tunnel with its twin bores each 64yd long. Two BR Standard Class 4 4-6-0s Nos 75071 and 75073, both shedded at Bath, haul the 2.45pm Bournemouth West to Bristol on a summer Saturday in the early 1950s.
The Late Ivo Peters

stone quarry and colliery sidings, while a short distance beyond was Emborough Quarry, followed by the 87yd Nettlebridge Viaduct. At Binegar were more stone quarry sidings and, for about 18 years, a 2ft 6in narrow gauge line to Oakhill Brewery. Between 1959 and 1966 calves were sent from this station to Scotland, one of the bankers being deputed to attach the vans to the rear of an afternoon train. Binegar was also the terminus of the 6.05pm from Bath, for many years the two-coach train being hauled by a tank engine, whereas until 1963 when BR Standard '4MT' 2-6-4Ts appeared, apart from this 6.05 working, tank engines had been rare on passenger trains on the northern section of the S&D, though common enough in the very early days.

At Binegar the banking engine picked up the banking key to allow it to return from Masbury Summit 'wrong line' to Binegar, there being no crossover at the summit. Using Whitaker's apparatus the banker collected the key from a catcher.

The fireman on one train engine looking out and seeing the apparatus ahead, quickly put out his own catcher, retrieved the banking key and proudly declared to his driver, 'I've got'n mate'. Realising his mistake, he threw the key off the engine, and the banker not having the necessary authority to return after completing its task, had to stop, leaving the train engine to struggle on without assistance.

A banking engine was normally required to be coupled to the brake van because a train needed assistance through several sections. If a banker had not been coupled and then failed, and if the main train had then passed a signalbox with its tail lamp showing, the signalman would have believed the train complete, signalled 'Off section' leaving the failed banker to be struck by the next train. If the type of brake van used had its body extended to the headstock, on reaching the summit at Masbury a guard

would use a special hook to uncouple the banker, afterwards hanging this hook on the smokebox door hand rail of the banker; but if the van had a platform at the end, this form of working was impossible and the train had to stop at Binegar for the guard to uncouple and replace the tail lamp on the brake van.

In the story told above, the driver not having received the banking key would have indicated this to the guard who would have uncoupled the banker.

Beyond Masbury Summit the line fell for eight miles to Evercreech Junction on a ruling gradient of 1 in 50 broken only by a short rise at Shepton Mallet. Below the summit was Masbury station, of different

Left:
Masbury Halt has a derelict appearance. View up the gradient of 1 in 50 towards the summit. *C. Steane*

31

design from the other Bath Extension stations. On the front wall of the station house was a stone-cut purporting to depict Masbury Castle. There was more than a little artistic licence about this engraving, for it portrayed a medieval castle in full panoply of drawbridge and portcullis, whereas the real castle was a much less sophisticated ancient British encampment. During World War 2 extensive sidings were laid to serve a United States Army camp east of the station. In clear weather extensive views were possible over the Vale of Avalon to the Quantocks and Exmoor.

The line crossed the 72yd long Hamwood Viaduct with quarry sidings either side of the track, access to which was controlled by Winsor Hill signalbox situated between Up and Down lines, and the only one on the Bath Extension built of stone. At Winsor Hill were separate tunnels, the Down line running through the original 239yd bore, and the Up through the 126yd tunnel cut when the line was doubled. Beyond was yet another quarry.

Approaching Shepton Mallet the Bath Road Viaduct, initially built to carry a single track, was later doubled. Early in 1946 one arch on the Down line became unsafe and single line working was introduced while scaffolding was erected for repairs. Then, during a February gale, the parapet and highest arch over the roadway collapsed. This arch, together with an adjoining one and the respective piers, was rebuilt, double line working being resumed in August. This viaduct was the highest on the line, having a maximum height of 62ft to the underside of the arch. The span of the largest arch was 50ft. From this viaduct could be seen extensive views over the town, the station itself being approached over the 308yd Charlton Viaduct.

Beyond Shepton Mallet station, which was situated on the eastern outskirts of the town and not so central as that of the GWR, the S&D passed under the GWR's Witham-Wells-Cheddar-Yatton branch and climbed

Left:
At Shepton Mallet the line descended to Charlton Road station across a 27-arch viaduct. BR Standard Class 4 4-6-0 No 75072 (83G, Templecombe) arrives with the 16.35 from Bath to Templecombe on 28 September 1965. Speed over the viaduct was restricted to 55mph. *John A. M. Vaughan*

Below:
Class 8F 2-8-0 No 48309 hauls the 'Wessex Downsman' an LCGB special, over Prestleigh Viaduct between Shepton Mallet and Evercreech New on 4 April 1965. The viaduct carried the line 121yd over a tributary brook of the River Alham. *R. Fisher*

to a mini-summit near Cannard's Grave. Passing through a cutting and under two twin arch bridges, the line wound down over an exposed hillside to Evercreech New station, much nearer the village than Evercreech Junction. This part of the line was notorious for its vulnerability to drifting snow. From Evercreech New to Evercreech Junction North signalbox was a short run of just over a mile. The branch line from Burnham and Highbridge joined just after passing the 56ft diameter turntable. Some of

Above:
Pecking Mill Viaduct, 60yd in length, consisting of four stone arches and a steel girder bridge over the A371, was patched and the retaining walls rebuilt in brick. This is one of the few structures still standing and recognisable in 1990, though the bridge beams have been removed. *C. Steane*

Right:
BR Standard Class 4MT 2-6-4T No 80037 at Evercreech Junction. Cans on the buffer beam are for supplying drinking water to the crossing keepers' lodges. *C. Steane*

the extensive sidings here were removed in 1964 when freight traffic slackened off. The passenger station was a third of a mile south of the actual junction. A tall stone water tower supplied water to the columns, one between the tracks opposite the station-master's house and the other at the north end of the Up platform. Most locomotives took on water here to be ready for the long climb over the Mendips, or across the fens to Highbridge.

The crossing cottages at Lamyatt and Bruton Road were SCR structures, and immediately south of the overbridge at Wyke Champflower was the physical junction between the SCR and the DCR. Away to the west just before Milepost 28, a turf-covered bank ran down towards the West of England main line. This was the site of a proposed broad gauge curve descending to join the Wilts, Somerset & Weymouth Railway. Beyond, the S&D crossed the WSWR. The station 'Cole for Bruton' was of DCR architecture with high gables and tall chimneys. Wincanton and Temple-combe Lower were of similar design and also in stone, whereas from Stalbridge southwards the stations were executed in red brick. The signalboxes south of Cole were of

Left:
Class 2P 4-4-0 No 40634 (83G Templecombe) and Class 9F 2-10-0 No 92006 on the Up 'Pines Express' leaving Evercreech Junction on 12 August 1961. The wagons standing on a level siding in the left background show that the passenger train is on a gradient. *G. W. Morrison*

Below left:
BR Standard Class 4 2-6-0 No 76025 heads the fast train of the day, the 1.10pm Bournemouth West to Bristol Temple Meads, away from Evercreech Junction on 7 September 1963. Behind the engine are the sidings and goods shed. The cattle loading dock is to the left of the smokebox. *D. A. Idle*

Below:
'Still-life' at Evercreech Junction: a branch line train for Highbridge waits to leave from the Up platform. Class 2 2-6-2T No 41296 shedded at Templecombe heads the 17.00 on 21 May 1965. Note the unusually tall signal post. There is a neat garden, tidy platform, no litter or graffiti – but where are the passengers? *R. F. Roberts*

Above:
In the fork between the single line of the branch and the doubled main line is the 56ft diameter turntable. A driver balanced his engine on the table, knocked the pin out of a bar which fell down and also unlocked the table. The crew pushed against this bar to turn the engine. If well balanced, once it started moving it could rotate three or four times. If unbalanced it was so stiff that the table had to be inched round with a pinch bar. *C. Steane*

Above right:
Class 3F 0-6-0 No 43218 (formerly S&D No 73) having brought in the branch line train from Highbridge, stands at the Down platform 1 June 1957. Between the widely spaced roads that once were broad gauge, stands a water column and a cast iron 'devil' which kept it from freezing in cold weather. The column was supplied by the water tower beyond the crossing gates over the A371. The change of gradient in the direction of Lamyatt Crossing is apparent in the hazy distance. *R. E. Toop*

Right:
On the Up platform stood a Victorian cast iron urinal elaborately decorated. At some time this was modestly shielded by concrete slabs and uprights emanating from Exmouth Junction concrete works. *C. Steane*

the low wooden LSWR pattern. The width of the embankments and the generous space between the Up and Down roads in this section of line hint that the earthworks were planned for broad gauge. Although the really steep gradients on the S&D ended at Evercreech Junction, the line again rose to a miniature summit at Wincanton. Here the platforms were staggered and at the far end of the layout a private siding led to Messrs Cow & Gate's factory.

After crossing the River Cale beyond Wincanton, the line ran straight across the flat country of Blackmore Vale giving an engine the oppportunity of a fast run. A short distance beyond Horsington Crossing it reached the old Templecombe No 3 Junction where there was the choice of

Left:
BR Standard Class 9F 2-10-0 No 92006 shedded at Bath Green Park leaves Evercreech Junction with the 7.35am Nottingham to Bournemouth West on 8 July 1961. Smoke and steam almost obscure the tall Down starting signal, but not the stonework and steel plates of the massive water tower. The original steam pump housed in the base of the tower was replaced in 1942 by one powered by electricity.
J. C. Haydon

Below:
Between Evercreech Junction and Cole the S&D crossed the GWR's West of England main line. There was never a connection here, though one was planned in the early days of the Somerset Central. *C. Steane*

Right:
Between Evercreech Junction and Wincanton the S&D traversed a countryside of low hills and valleys. The village and station of Cole is seen here on 16 August 1961 when Class 4F 0-6-0 No 44417 shedded at 82G Templecombe, hauls the 3.20pm Bath to Templecombe, a train run as a connection off the Down 'Pines Express'. By 1966 the goods siding, the signal, the trailing crossover between Up and Down lines and the timber-built signalbox had all been taken away. Above the first coach can be seen quite a few coal wagons, the merchant maybe taking advantage of stocking up at summer prices. Notice that the tender is much narrower than the coach. A grindstone stands at the rear of the permanent way hut while to the right are railwaymen's allotments.
The Late Derek Cross

Centre right:
A Down stopping train approaches Cole headed by Class 2P 4-4-0 No 40700 on 16 August 1961.
The Late Derek Cross

Bottom right:
The main station building at Wincanton with its canopied shelter stands on the Down platform. This December 1965 view was taken from a window of a Templecombe to Bath train. The stationmaster's office is in a timber hut added to the camera-side of the station. The chimney is of brick. A concrete footbridge is beyond. The turnout in the foreground leads from the Up line to the goods yard, whilst that further down is a crossover.
C. Steane

either running down to the engine shed and yard and the original Templecombe Lower station, or up to Templecombe No 2 Junction. In 1966 the stationmaster's house of the original Lower station, closed in 1887, still stood alongside the modern red brick locomotive depot. The signalbox at Templecombe No 2 Junction controlled entry to the double track to Templecombe Upper, the SR station; or the single track S&D line to the post-1887 Templecombe Lower and the south. Templecombe No 1 signalbox stood

by Templecombe Lower platform. As most trains called at Templecombe Upper, it meant that they either had to be drawn in backwards by another engine if travelling in the Up direction, or be drawn out in reverse if travelling Down. It was a requirement that a passenger train (apart from those designed for push-pull working) had an engine at its leading end. The coupling on and use of a second engine added to both time and expense. The extra locomotive was attached or detached at No 2 Junction. It was strange

that the economy was never made of making more use of Templecombe Lower which could have had its facilities improved.

The two-road timber building forming the 1877 engine shed at Templecombe survived until 1951 when it was reconstructed in brick. At the rear was a 50ft diameter turntable. The Southern Region coded the shed 71H, the WR altering it to 82G and later 83G. When it closed on 7 March 1966 the building was let for other use.

From Templecombe southwards to Blandford Forum the S&D was single track with passing loops and worked by the Electric Train Token. The gradients of these sections were easy along Blackmore Vale and the valley of the River Stour. Rich green pastures — copses — hedgerows — trees —

Left:
The lower platform at Templecombe: a BR Standard Class 4 4-6-0 No 75072 brings in the 11.46 semi-fast from Bournemouth West on a day in December 1965. Although the current timetable showed no stop at Templecombe, the train pulled up at the platform to allow an exchange of engine crews. The building on the left is the base of the water tower.
C. Steane

Below:
The S&D single line passes under the LSWR's West of England main line at Templecombe. Here BR Standard Class 4MT 2-6-0 No 76025 takes the 17.45 for Bournemouth West southwards on 19 April 1965. The semaphore controls the entrance to the section where the lower platform was placed just in sight beyond the overbridge. G. F. Gillham

Common Lane Crossing — cows grazing the rich green pastures — hedgerows — trees — a stream — Park Lane Crossing — a bridge over the A30 trunk road — all these flashed by before the train slowed to a stop by the single platform at Henstridge where there was no passing loop. Henstridge was famous for being the last S&D station to display an oval wooden board indicating to the travelling lineman whether or not the electrical apparatus in the signalbox was in working order.

Beyond Plott Lane Crossing immediately south of the station, Marsh Lane and South Mead Crossings, the line passed over the county boundary into Dorset. South of Stalbridge the S&D crossed first the River Lydden and the River Stour, and then cut across the neck of a meander loop in a cutting which opened out into Sturminster

Above:
Blandford Forum station shortly after the withdrawal of passenger service in March 1966, but before dilapidation and vandalism had damaged the buildings. The goods yard on the Down side had a large crane, the hook can be seen below the left-hand end of the unusually tall signalbox. Both platforms had canopied shelters, but the stone station building was on the Up platform out of sight to the right. *C. Steane*

Right:
One of the larger S&D engineering structures: the viaduct and bridge over the River Stour at Blandford. This was the bridge furthest downstream on the River Stour which was used by the S&D. Not surprisingly, it was also the widest. The steel girders are supported on brick abutments provided with flood arches. *C. Steane*

Newton station where the platforms were slightly staggered. A 20mph restriction was in force at the facing points. Stourpaine crossing loop and signalbox were opened in the early 1900s to break up the 5½-mile long block section between Sturminster and Blandford; between the wars the box was only open on summer Saturdays and closed entirely in 1951. Near Stourpaine & Durweston halt the railway used the gap between the Dorset Downs and Cranbourne Chase made by the River Stour.

The line passed through Blandford Forum, re-crossed the Stour and proceeded via Charlton Marshall and Spetisbury halts to Bailey Gate on the outskirts of Sturminster Marshall, the site of a milk depot. At Corfe Mullen the line divided; the direct route to Broadstone went right, and that to Wimborne, left.

Above:
Charlton Marshall halt, a typical SR concrete structure retained its nameboards, though there was little else to see in 1966. However, the concrete sleepers on the Down line are of interest as few of these were laid on the S&D. *C. Steane*

Left:
Class 4F 0-6-0 No 44102 shedded 82G Templecombe approaches Charlton Marshall with a freight for Poole on 6 January 1961. The concrete permanent way hut on the left was constructed in that shape in order that it could be transported on a wagon without fouling the loading gauge.
G. A. Richardson

At Broadstone S&D trains used LSWR/SR metals to Poole and Bournemouth. From Poole the line climbed at 1 in 60 to Parkstone and on to Branksome

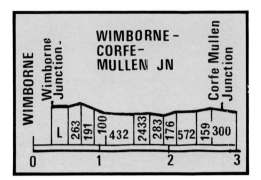

where the branch to Bournemouth West left the route to Bournemouth Central, a triangular junction being formed. Bournemouth West was the southern terminus of S&D trains until September 1965 when it was closed and services diverted to Central.

The two-road corrugated iron shed at Branksome was situated inside the triangular junction. A 50ft diameter turntable, latterly little used, was removed in the 1950s. Although busy, particularly on summer Saturdays, it never had its own locomotive allocation. Officially closed in January 1963, engines still made use of the yard until the sidings were taken out of use on 1 August 1965.

Right:
BR Standard Class 4MT 2-6-0
No 76010 at Bournemouth
Central. *C. Steane*

Below:
A milk train off the Highbridge
branch with tankers for London
via Templecombe approaches
Evercreech Junction double-
headed by ex-Midland Class 3F
0-6-0s Nos 43682 and 43436, the
latter engine being shedded at
Templecombe. The wagons with
tarpaulins stand on the Down
sidings between the branch and
main line, 17 June 1960.
J. A. Coiley

Highbridge branch

When the Highbridge line became a branch rather than the main line, some trains started at Evercreech Junction, others running through from Templecombe. At Evercreech Junction North signalbox the branch kept straight on and climbed at 1 in 144 towards the wooded country near Pylle. Immediately to the east of Pylle station the Fosse Way crossed the line, the overbridge being built sufficiently wide to allow for the double-tracked crossing loop. The loop was abolished in 1929 when the signalbox was reduced to a ground frame. Beyond, the line ran in a shallow wooded cutting under an overbridge, descending Pylle Bank on gradients of 1 in 115/100 to the low-lying ground of Pilton Park below Pennard Hill. It ran on an embankment and through another shallow cutting underneath the Shepton Mallet to Glastonbury road bridge immediately before West Pennard station. Here the station buildings, layout and immediate environment were similar to

Left:
Ex-GWR '2251' class 0-6-0 No 3215 taking a morning train from Evercreech Junction to Highbridge past West Pennard signalbox on 27 March 1961. This branch line station with passing loop and sidings had a considerable length of rodding to be kept in order. The roof of the substantial goods shed can be seen above the first coach. The timber hut to the right of the engine stabled a motor-powered permanent way trolley. Chairs and sleepers stored nearby. The guard and signalman are having a word. *Michael J. Fox*

Below:
West Pennard in 1966. The station building stands on the Up platform, right. Opposite on the Down side were a platform shelter and the large stone-walled goods shed with crane inside. Another crane stood outside in the yard. The stone base of the demolished signalbox is on the right. Lifting the Down track removed the only crossing loop between Evercreech Junction and Glastonbury. The barrow crossing now leads to nowhere. Beyond the road bridge is the commencement of Pylle Bank. *C. Steane*

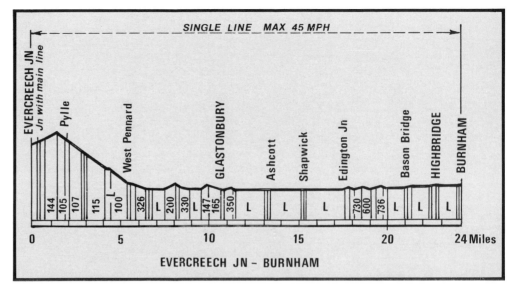

SINGLE LINE   MAX 45 MPH

EVERCREECH JN – BURNHAM

EVERCREECH JN *Jn with main line* · Pylle · West Pennard · GLASTONBURY · Ashcott · Shapwick · Edington Jn · Bason Bridge · HIGHBRIDGE · BURNHAM

144 105 107 115 L 100 326 L 200 330 L 147 165 350 L L L L 730 600 736 L L L

0   5   10   15   20   24 Miles

Pylle, though West Pennard's crossing loop lasted until 26 August 1964.

The line ran straight and almost level for 3½ miles to the Wells-Glastonbury road overbridge. To the south, Glastonbury Tor and its medieval church tower stood above the willows and waterlogged cattle pastures of Queen's Sedgemoor. Just over half a mile beyond the bridge the branch from Wells ran in alongside. When Wells Branch Junction signalbox closed on 2 December 1878, the branch was extended to Glastonbury parallel with the Highbridge line.

Glastonbury, one-time S&D headquarters, had a three-road station, Wells branch trains using the outer face of the island platform. The footbridge was unusual in latterly having open lattice sides, yet being roofed and with windows above the latticework. The booking hall and stationmaster's office were on the Up platform at the far end of which stood the signalbox.

From Glastonbury the line ran westward across heathland for 2½ miles to Ashcott & Meare halt. Hereabouts were peat workings, some of which supplied traffic for the

Left:
The forecourt of Glastonbury station, 1967. The covered footbridge has windows to give light to the stairs. Covered parcels loading bay. Line in foreground crosses road to sawmill on right off the edge of the picture. *C. Steane*

Below:
Ashcott & Meare was a single platform halt, another product of Exmouth Junction concrete depot. Even the station nameboard is precast concrete. At the far right is the red brick and tiled station building; on the left the wooden hut with ground frame for working the protecting home signals. *C. Steane*

railway. One such bog was served by Petfu [peat fuel] siding. Onwards towards the passing loop at Shapwick there were heaths and peat workings on both sides of the line; alders, willows, ditches and drains being the characteristics of these Somerset levels. The signalbox at Shapwick controlled sections from Glastonbury to Edington. The modern concrete platforms from the Exmouth Junction Works contrasted strongly with quaint oil lamps. The line ran over the flat lands of Westcott Heath, Catcott Heath, Edington Heath to the level crossing and former junction station at Edington Burtle. The bay platform for the former Bridgwater branch still remained in the 1960s although the track was lifted after closure of the branch in 1954, passenger services ceased in 1952. Beyond the station, the line crossed the River Brue and ran past the Unigate Creamery to Bason Bridge halt just beyond.

At Highbridge, once the company's headquarters, in the 1960s the former locomotive and carriage works were still *in*

situ to the south of the line, looking much as they did when closed 35 years previously. These quite extensive buildings provided for all the engineering needs of the S&D — sawmill, boiler shop, foundry, machine shop, spring shop, paint shop, carriage and wagon shop, stores and drawing office. Although Highbridge was so well equipped and used workmen whose skills were famous as far afield as Canada, with the exception of three small tank engines no new locomotives were ever built. Its work was concerned with overhauling and rebuilding. One curiosity was that it had no road access, everything having to arrive or leave by rail. The works was used by the Government during World War 2, but the former carriage and wagon erecting shop was burnt down in the 1950s.

Highbridge running shed was a four-road affair of brick, built alongside the works paint shop and was the last S&D shed to use Midland 0-4-4Ts, a type in use on the line from 1876 until 1956. Modern improvements to the depot included an asbestos

Below:
Alexander's Siding: Eclipse Peat Company's crossing near Ashcott, 30 October 1956.
Colin G. Maggs

Left:
Class 2MT 2-6-2Ts No 41307 and 41269 passing Catcott on their way from Evercreech Junction to Highbridge with the LCGB special Saturday 5 March 1966.
The Late Ivo Peters

Below:
Ex-GWR 0-6-0 No 3218 near Catcott with the 4.00pm local from Highbridge, October 1964.
The Late Ivo Peters

Above:
Edington Burtle: the former Up platform now used for all traffic. The canopy supported by two rows of posts and the small station building are the remnants of Edington Junction. Bridgwater trains departed from the bay on the right. Glastonbury trains used the Down platform, removed when the crossing loop and signalbox were taken out in 1956. A solitary oil lamp hung from the roof outside the waiting room. The finial and barge boards give a pleasing touch to the canopy which looks as though it has not seen paint for a long time. Notice the central water channel in the platform.
C. Steane

Centre right:
At the milk depot adjacent to Bason Bridge halt Class 4F 0-6-0 No 44272 marshals tank wagons on 18 May 1963. The Western Region diverted milk traffic to run to London via Highbridge rather than via Templecombe.
R. E. Toop

Right:
Bason Bridge halt with milk depot beyond the crossing gates. *C. Steane*

54

coaling shelter added in the mid-1950s. Although officially closed on 11 May 1959, locomotives continued to be stabled in the shed overnight, including ex-GWR '2251' class 0-6-0s which latterly worked branch trains. Curiously enough ex-GWR 0-6-0 No 3218 replaced ex-S&D 0-6-0 No 43218.

In 1965 Highbridge station seemed too large for the few branch services using it as a terminus: one S&D platform would have sufficed, yet four were available. One of the most interesting and remarkable features at Highbridge was the crossing, on the level, of

the GWR's Bristol-Exeter main line. This crossing, for which there were complex signalling arrangements in order to avoid dangerous conflicting movements, allowed the S&D to run another 1½ miles to Burnham-on-Sea. After the Burnham and Highbridge Wharf lines had been closed, the crossing was altered on 16 May 1965 to enable milk still to be taken from Bason Bridge creamery by rail, a direct connection being made from the S&D line to the ex-GWR goods yard on the west side of the Up line so that the crossing still remained.

Above:
Ivatt Class 2MT 2-6-2T No 41307 leaving Highbridge with the 14.18 to Templecombe on 28 December 1965.
Michael J. Fox

Above:
Ex-GWR 0-6-0 No 2250 crosses the main GWR line after taking wagons to the S&D exchange sidings at Highbridge, 3 June 1954. *F. J. Saunders*

Right:
Ex-GWR 0-6-0 No 3210 en route for Burnham having passed Highbridge East 'A' signalbox. Highbridge Wharf sidings are behind the photographer. *Photographer not known*

Beyond, on the Burnham line, was High-bridge East goods depot and further on Highbridge Wharf sidings, surprisingly extensive and stretching for about a third of a mile alongside the River Brue. As well as serving shipping, the sidings gave access to Bland's sawmill, the West Somerset Co-op and Highbridge Anthracite Fuel Works. Further west towards Burnham were sidings to three brick works. Burnham station, adjacent to the sea, was most conveniently situated for day trippers. The original platform was covered by a brick-built train shed, but the longer excursion platform was without this facility. During the period when steamer services were operated to South Wales, a line continued on to a steeply graded pier beyond.

Wells branch

Passenger trains for the 5½-mile run to Wells left from the outer face of the island platform at Glastonbury and ran on a separate single track parallel with the Evercreech Junction line until diverging a mile from Glastonbury. A low bank and a line of willows marks the site of the line across Crannel Moor towards Polsham. At one point the line, closed in 1951, crossed a farm road and in 1967, a solitary concrete post which had supported the crossing gate alone remained to reveal that a railway had been laid there.

At Polsham a house has been built across the former track bed opposite the wicket gate and concrete level crossing posts. By

Above:
Class 3F 0-6-0 No 43427 at Burnham-on-Sea 22 August 1959 with the 1.20pm SO local from Evercreech Junction. Although passenger services were generally withdrawn between Highbridge and Burnham in 1951, an occasional train used it during the period of the summer timetable. A 'Black and White Motorways' Cheltenham coach stands on the left. *R. E. Toop*

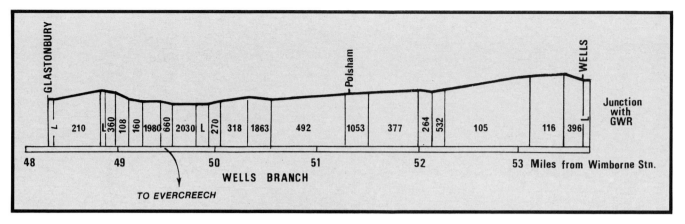

GLASTONBURY

Polsham

WELLS

Junction
with
GWR

| L | 210 | L | 360 | 108 | 160 | 1980 | 660 | 2030 | L | 270 | 318 | 1863 | 492 | 1053 | 377 | 264 | 532 | 105 | 116 | 396 | L |

48   49   50   51   52   53 Miles from Wimborne Stn.

WELLS BRANCH

TO EVERCREECH

Above:
Gradient profile of the Wells branch.

Below:
The former Polsham station seen from the level crossing. View towards Wells. *C. Steane*

the mid-1960s the site of the branch was covered with long grass and blackberry bushes, but the single platform and brick buildings of Polsham halt could be recognised and in 1967 were still occupied by the family which had supplied the crossing keepers for 30 years prior to the line's closure.

Beyond Polsham, as the branch approached the foot of Mendip and the city of Wells, it ran into hilly country. A substantial stone bridge with abutments carried a minor road over the single line. By 1967 the former track formation and cutting had been taken in and cultivated as part of the garden of Coxley Farm. Either side of Coxley Crossing the line ran in a cutting. The keeper's cottage still displayed the

nameboard, but washing hung out to dry over what was once the railway — reminiscent of a scene in the film *Oh Mr Porter*. More scrub and blackberry bushes line the sides of the cutting.

Approaching Wells the line rose on a gradient of 1 in 105 for a mile, before it curved into a shallow cutting before running into Priory Road station. Two other railway companies reached Wells: the East Somerset Railway (ESR) from Shepton Mallet had its station only a few chains east of that of the SCR, while the B&E's Cheddar Valley line used Tucker Street station a few chains to the west. The B&E and the ESR were eventually connected by a line crossing part of the S&D's goods depot using nine chains of S&D metals. After GWR trains had run

Above:
A substantial stone bridge with abutments carried a lane over the line at Coxley. By 1967 the former track bed was being cultivated as part of the garden of Coxley Farm. *C. Steane*

Left:
Crossing keeper's cottage at Coxley, view towards Glastonbury. *C. Steane*

Above:
S&D pull-and-push coaches at Wells, Priory Road: 'PL & PH' can be seen at the bottom left-hand end panel of the coach. Notice the train shed and the three S&DJR fire buckets hanging on the wall. View east.
Lens of Sutton

Below right:
Wells, Priory Road. View west early in 1967 after the removal of the train shed. 15mph limit sign. *C. Steane*

non-stop through Priory Road for 56 years, it was decided that they should call to facilitate transfer and make rail travel a little more convenient to people living in that area of the city. When the S&D track was lifted, lines at Priory Road were left *in situ* because they were used by Yatton to Witham trains.

The two-road stone-built locomotive shed at Wells was noted for the fact that its water supply was raised to the tower by a pump driven by a water wheel made in the locomotive works at Highbridge in 1861. Although the engine shed technically closed in 1947, it remained open as a stabling point until the line's closure in 1951.

Bridgwater branch

From the bay platform at Edington Junction, Bridgwater trains curved across a drain and over a level crossing, no gradients being experienced over Chilton Moor. After a

Above:
Wells, Priory Road in the spring of 1967 after the demolition of the passenger station showing the large and substantial S&D goods shed.   *C. Steane*

Left:
Cossington station on 29 August 1956. View towards Edington.
Colin G. Maggs

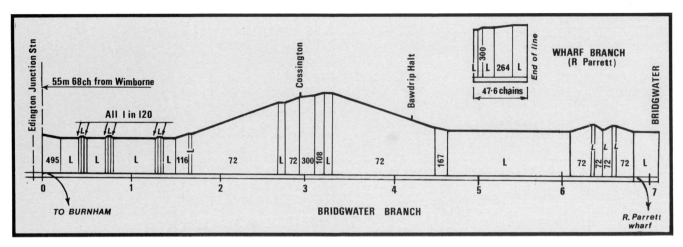

Edington Junction Stn

55m 68ch from Wimborne

All 1 in 120

Cossington

Bawdrip Halt

300   264   End of line

WHARF BRANCH
(R Parrett)

47·6 chains

BRIDGWATER

TO BURNHAM

495   L   L   L   L   116   72   L   72   300   108   L   72   167   L   72   72   72   72   L

BRIDGWATER BRANCH

R. Parrett
wharf

Above:
Gradient profile of the
Bridgwater branch.

mile it tackled a gradient of 1 in 116 and soon steepened to 1 in 72 in order to pass over the Polden Hills. The rising gradient eased to 1 in 300 at Cossington which was provided with a single siding and cattle pens. A quarter of a mile beyond was a short level stretch before the descent at 1 in 72. Midway down was Bawdrip halt

opened in October 1923 and another example of Exmouth Junction concrete. At the foot of the incline the S&D traversed Horsey Level on the flat apart from gradients of 1 in 72 across the GWR main line and the A38 Bristol-Bridgwater road. A siding led off to Wild's Cement Works.

Above right:
An Up train hauled by a '1P' 0-4-4T approaching Bawdrip halt. The bare platform opened on 7 July 1923, a shelter being added the following year.
Lens of Suttons

Right:
Bridgwater North, 29 August 1956.   *Colin G. Maggs*

Although the branch itself closed in 1954, the passenger station remained in use, but as a British Road Services depot. The façade of red brick relieved by yellow brick around windows and doors, had six bays giving access to an island-type platform covered by an awning for much of its length. In the goods yard was a red brick goods shed. The yard remained in use after closure of the rest of the line to Edington, access being by a chord line opened on 27 June 1954 from the GWR's Bridgwater Docks branch, the yard being finally closed in April 1967. The track at the S&D's own Bridgwater Wharf had been lifted in January 1942. The single road red brick engine shed had its access across a 50ft diameter turntable. The shed closed shortly after the end of World War 1.

WESTERN **BRITISH RAILWAYS** REGION

Permanent withdrawal of Passenger Train Service
EDINGTON JUNCTION TO BRIDGWATER NORTH

ON AND FROM

MONDAY, 1st DECEMBER, 1952

THE PASSENGER TRAIN SERVICE

BETWEEN

EDINGTON JUNCTION
AND BRIDGWATER NORTH

WILL BE WITHDRAWN PERMANENTLY

The 8.0 a.m. train Glastonbury and Street to Edington Junction will cease to run on the same date

The existing services of collection and delivery of passenger rated traffic (Parcels, Luggage, etc.) will be maintained from Bridgwater General Station. Such traffic may be collected by the Public or accepted for despatch during the normal hours of business at Bridgwater General and Edington Junction Stations.

Paddington Station, W.2.
October, 1952

K. W. C. GRAND,
Chief Regional Officer.

E9—612   Bartlett & Son, 138, Cowick Street, Exeter.

Left:
Handbill announcing withdrawal of passenger service Edington Junction to Bridgwater North.

63

3

Railwaymen's reminiscences

The S&D was above all a friendly line. It was not so large that it was impersonal; it was sufficiently small for people to know each other. It was worked efficiently, yet there was usually time for a short chat. Men who had experience in industry said that they found workers much more friendly on the railway than in a factory. More help would be given to others — perhaps you would dispose of someone's engine so that they could have a drink before the pubs closed, whereas working in industry there was more cut and thrust with far less give and take.

Fred Epps drove the longest-ever fitted train from Poole to Templecombe, 26 vehicles and although close coupled, there was still a certain amount of slack and he had to drive with care in order to avoid snatches. He had driven a Class 8F 2-8-0 light engine from Branksome to Poole Yard and was going to have 20 vans, but the guard came up to him and said 'The foreman wants to know if you'll take the rest'. Fred replied, 'How many?' and received the reply 'Half a dozen'. 'Oh, all right, I'll do it to help out; but tell him he must get the signalman at Broadstone to let me have his distant signal off because I don't want to have to stop on the 1 in 75 bank with this lot.' The agreement worked and the train successfully reached Templecombe.

The northern end of the line being hilly led to operating problems. Following the disaster on 20 November 1929 when the crew of S&D 2-8-0 No 89 were overcome by fumes in Combe Down Tunnel, and, lying unconscious, were unable to apply the brakes down the bank into Bath with the result that it derailed in Bath goods yard, the authorities decided that to help prevent a repetition, they would use coal with less sulphur content. Instead of Bath's supply being north coal, it was changed to Welsh.

Devonshire and Combe Down Tunnels, 447yd and 1,829yd in length respectively, were both single line bores, the first on a gradient of 1 in 50 and the second on 1 in 100. Smoke issuing from the chimney of an engine climbing the gradient was forced up

to the roof of the tunnel and then driven downwards by the draught, resulting in the footplatemen having to breathe foul sulphurous fumes which were quite bad enough even with Welsh coal. On a humid day when the air was still, a crew would dip their wipers in a bucket of cold water and place them over their faces. Even in the relatively short Devonshire Tunnel drivers and firemen sometimes had to kneel on the footplate to seek the coolest and freshest air. On emerging into daylight in Lyncombe Vale it was quite common for an engine to be saturated with condensed moisture which dried out leaving a coating of yellow sulphur.

In the Up direction Combe Down Tunnel could cause a fireman considerable concern because he knew that in half or three-quarters of an hour's time his engine would be disposed of and therefore he had to let the fire burn down or lose face in the estimation of the shed staff. Whether working a fast train like the 'Pines', or a goods train, as he approached Radstock coming down from the Mendips, he took his irons and levelled the fire, so apart from an emergency, avoided any more firing. If, as he approached Combe Down Tunnel, he felt that the engine required more fuel, the shovel was used as quickly as possible after passing through Midford in order to make no smoke in the tunnel itself.

One day Bill Rawles had Class 7F 2-8-0 No 53806 with a load of 66 empty wagons from Evercreech Junction to Bath. He was assisted by a banker to Binegar where he shunted off six wagons, the capacity of the siding at Bath being limited to 60. He struggled to Midford where he gave the engine full regulator. A quarter of a mile inside the tunnel No 53806 slipped to a standstill. Two cattle wagons loaded with cows had been placed next to the engine — they should not have been — and the heat and the noise made them bellow. Bill Rawles set back to the telephone at the tunnel mouth. Percy Savage at Midford box answered, 'What's the trouble?' The problem was explained and he gave permission

Tablets and the Whitaker Tablet Exchange Apparatus

The tablet allowing access to a single line section could be picked up at speed by the Whitaker tablet exchange apparatus, a far more humane method than a fireman carrying out this by hand and sustaining a bruised arm. The normal apparatus was turned at right angles to the track in order to make a catch, the impact on collection turning the arm away from the train to give the necessary margin of clearance. In places where space was limited, such as between tracks, a 'falling man' type was used, and instead of being swung, the apparatus fell into a sump.

Left:
Tablet in leather pouch placed on catcher at Midford ready to be collected by Up train. *C. Steane*

Right:
Tablet catcher on lineside post at Corfe Mullen. Apparatus in safety position. *C. Steane*

Facing page, top:
'Falling man' type catcher at Bath Junction. Apparatus in safety position. Catcher jaws can be seen on right. *C. Steane*

Facing page, bottom:
The catcher fixed to the tender of Class 7F 2-8-0 No 53809 for use when travelling tender-first. The catcher's jaws face the direction of travel. Note the rubber block at the rear of the catcher to soften the blow of the tablet after being caught. Picture taken in Woodham's scrapyard, Barry, late spring 1966. *C. Steane*

Right:
Tyer's No 6 electric tablet apparatus in Midford signalbox.
C. Steane

Below right:
Leather pouches for holding tablets hanging in Midford signalbox like Lilliputian mailbags. *C. Steane*

Facing page, above left:
If an engine was not fitted with Whitaker's apparatus, or it was malfunctioning, exchange had to be by hand. In this event a pouch with a larger loop was used. Fireman picking up tablet from the signalman at Bath Junction. *C. Steane*

Facing page, above right:
Signalman Harry Wiltshire catches tablet from fireman of Down train at Midford. *C. Steane*

Facing page, bottom:
Midford signalman Percy Savage holds up S&D pilotman armband. In the event of a tablet being lost, or a malfunction of Tyer's apparatus, pilotman working was instituted. Instead of a train having a tablet as an authority to proceed on a single line, the fact of having a pilotman aboard gave the authority. *C. Steane*

for the train to return down the gradient to Midford. A bank engine was sent from Bath and piloted him in and even with its help, difficulty was experienced ascending the gradient. On arrival at Bath, Bill tested the sand and found it was not working, though it had functioned perfectly when he set out. He attributed the problem to the sand getting wet.

Radstock coal clinkered very badly and if burning it, three or four buckets of limestone had to be put down on the firebars as a base to prevent the clinker adhering. The Radstock engines used limestone all the time and their fires required cleaning every two banking trips. Large lumps of limestone were provided and if these were too big and required breaking with a hammer, firemen found it easier to use some ballast which was the right size.

Welsh coal was economical, a Dorset '7' could take a full load on a journey of 26 miles each way to Evercreech Junction and back which included steep banks, yet on an average would not burn more than three tons of Welsh coal, whereas north coal burnt like paper. Bedwas was the favourite Welsh coal and using it one could go from Bath to Templecombe and back without resorting to the clinker bar.

Coaling at Bath was by a steel trolley which held about half a ton. A man filled it by hand, then wheeled it across the stage and tipped it into a chute where it slid down into the tender. No more than six or seven loads were required to refill. The only disadvantage with Welsh coal was that because it broke easily it could not be tipped mechanically like the harder north coal and so a monetary saving by mechanising the procedure could not be made. Welsh coal being very dusty needed a greater supply of primary air through the ashpan. Dust was never shovelled on unless the fire was burning well and the engine moving because otherwise it would have choked the fire.

Most railwaymen were scrupulously honest, but one driver on the Highbridge branch once stole two ducks from a farm. Their owner, suspecting that an engineman was responsible, reported the matter to the police and two detectives awaited the errant driver at Evercreech Junction. They searched the engine but could find no trace of the missing birds and had to go away empty-handed. And where were the ducks? In their natural element of course — swimming in the tender's water tank.

At the head of a significant gradient the GWR had a notice requiring goods and mineral trains to stop and pin down brakes, but the S&D relied on the skill of a locomotive crew and guard to keep a train under control with just the engine, tender and van brakes, though very occasionally some S&D drivers stopped and had the wagon brakes pinned down. An S&D guard could never sit down for long as he was continually turning his brake on or off, as for example between Midford and Radstock, his 60-wagon train may have been on three differing gradients and it was his duty to prevent wagons from bumping into the engine, a task made harder by the wagons having free-running oil axleboxes rather than the old-fashioned grease pattern. S&D guards were tested on the rules every six months and if they did not know them thoroughly, were sent back to the yard as shunters. When the S&D closed and guards were transferred to former GWR lines, they found that they were rarely tested on their knowledge of the Rule Book.

One ex-S&D guard working a loaded 50-wagon mineral train down Stapleton Road bank into Bristol had the brakes on his ex-GWR van red hot. An ex-GWR signalman, not used to this sight, believed that the brake van was on fire and phoned the next box for the train to be stopped. A goods train had to be taken slowly downhill. If it ran out of control a driver was tempted to apply the brakes fully, but this would lock the wheels and then he would have to ease the brake off to let them turn again before re-applying the shoes. Drivers dropped sand to guard against the wheels 'picking up' on a descent. Some drivers misused the brakes as they enjoyed seeing fire come from them if applied fiercely at speed. The Dorset '7s' had Ferodo brake blocks which lasted some time, but Class 8F 2-8-0s had standard cast iron blocks which were worn out after one trip from Bath to Evercreech Junction and back. The Dorset '7s' had a steam brake cylinder for the leading pair of driving wheels (this also worked the brakes on the pony truck in earlier years) and steam brake cylinders under both the fireman's and driver's side for braking the intermediate, driving and trailing wheels (ie three brake cylinders on each engine), plus a steam brake cylinder on the tender. A Class 8F only had one steam brake cylinder on the engine and one on the tender, the difference in braking ability was quite noticeable.

Class 7F tyres were riveted on whereas those of Class 8F were only shrunk on. One '8F' driver having run into Bath with a heavy train was proceeding along the goods loop between Bath Junction and Bath Goods, when he heard a clanking noise. Looking out he noticed that a tyre had come off a driving wheel due to the heat caused by the brake blocks, the wheel actually running round inside the tyre. When the locomotive was examined at Bath shed, it was found that nearly all the tyres had shifted.

Crossing Gates

As much of the countryside over which the original Somerset Central and Dorset Central line ran was level and rural while rail and road traffic were both light, crossing gates were a familiar feature of the S&D. Bridges would have been more expensive necessitating either road or rail having to be raised and then lowered to gain height for one to bridge the other. In later years with the increase in road transport they were inconvenient obstructions particularly across the A367 at Radstock and the A371 at Evercreech Junction.

Left:
The large and substantial crossing gates across the A371 at Evercreech Junction worked by the signalman from the adjacent box. Cross-braced timbers support the wire mesh. When closed, red warning discs and lamps faced traffic. The gates are hinged on stout steel posts.
C. Steane

Below:
Worked by a crossing keeper resident in the nearby cottage were long, single gates suspended by rods and wires from a supporting post. This was at Lamyatt Crossing on the main line south of Evercreech Junction. *C. Steane*

Right:
On the Highbridge branch were
single gates; the ones shown
here at Cemetery Lane east of
Glastonbury. *C. Steane*

Below right:
The outdoor ground frame at
Elbow Corner Crossing; left lever
Up home, right Down home.
C. Steane

The 12.10am, nicknamed the 'Ghost Train', was the heaviest of the day, taking Avonmouth traffic, which was all weighty, to Templecombe. When working an unfitted train such as this, it was common practice to shut the vacuum ejector down, hook the vacuum brake up and use the straight steam brake. Several times a Class 8F driver has applied its steam brake at Masbury, the fireman wound the tender brake on as hard as he could, yet the train ran away down through Shepton, Evercreech New and Evercreech Junction. If you knew you were out of control passing Evercreech Junction North distant, you sounded a long whistle to warn the signalman at Evercreech Junction South to open the crossing gates at the far end of the station. If a train ran out of control through Evercreech Junction and stopped beyond, the signalman called it back with a white or green light.

On at least one occasion the 12.10am had braking assistance from Binegar to Evercreech Junction. This banker had assisted the Up Mail from Evercreech Junction to Binegar and was waiting to return light. As '7F' No 53803 with the 12.10 had 46 heavily-loaded vehicles and had already lost 15min between Radstock and Chilcompton, the driver wisely asked for braking assistance. The Mail banker was coupled in front of the '7F' and the vacuum brakes connected. At Masbury summit the regulators were closed, the handbrakes screwed down and the driver on the leading locomotive definitely applied the vacuum brake fully for the crew of No 53803 saw their gauge go to zero. Nevertheless that train ran away down over the Mendips and did not come to a halt until a quarter of a mile beyond Evercreech Junction station. The brake van was partly alight due to fire coming off the brake blocks and igniting its floor. The '7F' did not escape scot-free. Its blocks were so worn down that she had to be taken to Templecombe Lower to have new ones fitted before she could return to Bath.

Prior to being fitted with Ferodo brake blocks, cast iron ones on Dorset '7s' going down from the Mendips to Evercreech Junction glowed so hot that 'you could see rabbits playing in the fields'. One driver told me, 'It just wasn't done to pin down brakes on the S&D. There was no time between passenger trains to stop and pin down brakes and then release them. I've been on the turntable at Evercreech Junction and seen trains coming down the bank. It's been like a Brock's Benefit Night with fire and flames coming off the loco and tender wheels, and all the guard's wheels and blocks red hot. Sheets of flame; great Catherine wheels.'

For years S&D management refused to allow fitted vehicles and the vacuum brake

to be operated. This was because of the potential hazard in the event of a train being banked say from Evercreech Junction to Masbury and then a snatch causing the couplings to break on the dip near Shepton Mallet and automatically applying the vacuum brake. The wagons at the front would stop and the banker, unaware of what was happening, would continue to push its way towards them, forcing intervening wagons off the rails. This ban was eased when the Southern Region took over and freight trains on the Dorset could be run partly fitted. Shunters at Bath were told that they must shunt vacuum-fitted vehicles next

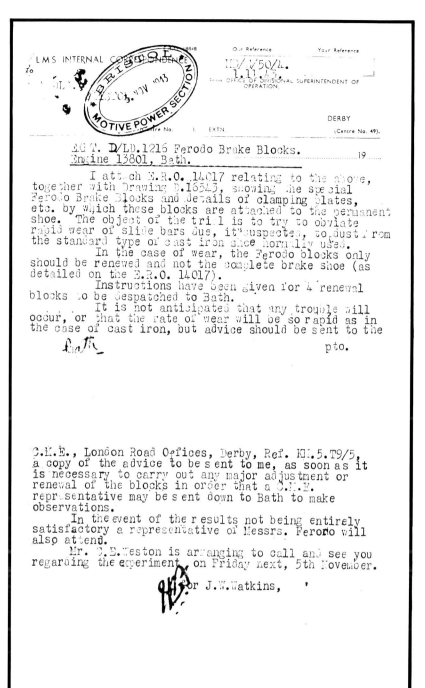

Above:
Internal correspondence from the Divisional Locomotive Superintendent, Bristol, economically typed on both sides of a small sheet of paper during World War 2. It refers to the initial trial of Ferodo brake blocks on S&D Class 7F 2-8-0 No 13801.

Water

One problem faced by the S&D operating authorities was the maintenance of adequate water supplies for their engines. At several stations, Evercreech Junction and Sturminster Newton for example, they built a water tower supporting a tank, a pump in the base of the tower keeping the tank full. At Sturminster Newton locomotives were filled by means of a hosebag direct from the tank, while at Evercreech Junction engines took their supply from a water crane.

Right:
Water crane at Evercreech Junction replenishing the tender of Class 8F 2-8-0 No 48706 on 6 March 1966. *C. Steane*

Facing page, top:
Fire buckets were prominent accessories outside inflammable buildings such as signalboxes. Here is a selection outside Midford box. *C. Steane*

Facing page, bottom:
Water tank at Sturminster Newton. Notice that the stove chimney is cunningly taken round the base of the tank to stop the water freezing in low temperatures. *C. Steane*

74

to the locomotive, connect up the pipes and have the brake tested. BR Standard Class 5 4-6-0s were considered very good engines, but were not so good at braking a freight train as a 'Black Five', in fact the Southern Region stipulated that Standard '5s' must have two fitted vans behind the tender to assist with the braking. One S&D driver, surprised at the relatively poor efforts of a Standard '5' at stopping, found that the required two vans were merely piped, having no brakes of their own.

Frank Staddon was the guard of a train carrying eight Churchill tanks, a Class 7F 2-8-0 and a Class 4 0-6-0 double-heading it all the way from Wool on the Dorchester to Poole line. At Evercreech Junction, Frank asked for a banker up to Masbury and was told by the shunter: 'No you can't have one because you've got two engines'. Frank insisted, 'I want a banker in case of a breakaway because my brake won't hold that weight'. The shunter argued, 'Well, the wagons are vacuum fitted so they wouldn't run away'. Frank inquired, 'What about brake failure?' The shunter still refused him a banker so Control was phoned. They agreed to Frank's wise request.

One guard thought that he would play a trick on the Shepton Mallet signalman so just before his van passed the box one night, took off the tail lamp, hid it in his van and then replaced it shortly beyond. The alert signalman correctly noticed its absence and rang through to Binegar for the train to be stopped. The Binegar 'bobby' came up and said, 'Guard, I believe your tail lamp is out'. 'Is it?' expressed the guard with feigned surprise, 'I am sorry, I thought it was burning all right. But if you say it's out, we'll go and have a look . . . Yes, it's alight all right'. The Binegar signalman rang his colleague at Shepton and told him he needed glasses because the light was burning perfectly.

Winsor Hill Tunnel was an especially bad place for blowbacks unless precautions were taken, as Down trains often entered the single bore at 60mph. The sudden force of air sometimes caused the cab floorboards to come up, Class 2P 4-4-0s being particularly prone to this trouble.

Priming could cause problems. A fireman preparing his engine at Bath turned the injector on and then went off to get another engine ready, completely forgetting the state of the boiler on the first. His driver going round oiling failed to notice that the injector was on and when the time came for them to leave the shed, the engine went on hydraulic power rather than steam. Black, sooty water poured from the chimney and seemed to go everywhere. They passed over Victoria Bridge Road on this beautiful summer's day.

The next morning, Shedmaster Harold Morris called the driver over and said that he had received a letter of complaint from a lady who had been passing on her way to the park dressed in a light-coloured summer frock and had been drenched with sooty water. BR had to pay her claim.

A Class 5 with 12 coaches stopped at Blandford for water, quite a tricky procedure as the gradient fell, was then level, followed by a rise. While the tank was being filled the guard went up to the driver and said that a woman had complained that the jerk when stopping had caused a case to fall off the luggage rack on top of her. From then onwards, that driver, in order to stop more smoothly, used a trick that he had learned from another driver when refreshing himself on the Gloucester to Birmingham road. He opened the large ejector for a while before applying the brake — not considered good practice, but certainly producing a smoother stop.

Some railwaymen had free allotments alongside the S&D. One such piece of land worked by a guard was not far from the Victoria Brick Works siding on the 1 in 50 gradient out of Bath. When the brick works was open it provided him with water, a rotary pump worked by a handle driving water along piping. When the works closed, this source of supply finished so the guard had to look around for another. He managed to persuade returning banking engines to stop and give him water, though a driver was reluctant to stay long and looking at his watch would say, 'I'll have to go, I'm two minutes late already'. One season this guard suspected someone of stealing his hard-won water so he tipped some weed-killer into his tank. The row of beans on an adjoining plot died shortly afterwards.

A guard at Evercreech Junction was boasting that his watch was both shock-proof and waterproof. A driver looking at it and hoping to take him down a peg or two tossed it into the tender water tank saying, 'Well, let's test it then!'

A 2½hr break between the last down train at 12.10am and the Down Mail at 2.40am gave the signalman on duty at Midford a chance to take a rest on the locker. One night, half asleep, the signalman there was surprised to hear chains rattling. His confidence was not boosted when he heard a thump, thump, thump on the door and looking up saw a face framed by white hair staring at him through the window. He was scared, thinking it the Devil himself. This eerie figure asked, 'Have you seen my two goats?'

The SR 'West Country' Pacifics were liked by S&D drivers for their good steaming, comfort, protection from the weather and the convenience of electric light — for on the Mendips the wind in winter often used to blow out the gauge lamps and headlamps. A signalman was required to stop a train if a headlamp was not lit and if still windy, it was difficult to light it *in situ* and it had to be taken into the cab.

On tight curves between Wellow and Writhlington a 'West Country' would slip at 60-70mph. They used 30 pints of oil in preparation, whereas a Midland 0-4-4T only needed four pints. 'West Countries' wasted most of their oil spilling it out round sharp curves. In preparing a 'West Country' a fireman might need 10 buckets of sand to fill the boxes, compared to three or four for a Class 5. A driver had to keep his eye on the steam chest pressure gauge and if he kept it below the 90lb reading, it would rarely slip on starting.

One driver confessed, 'We had an illegal dodge. We made a brake hook out of a 6in split pin — these were normally used on the brake blocks. We straightened out this pin and then put it over the top of the brake. It curved down and you bent it round to go under the fulcrum rod. We made sure it was tight, then we turned the vacuum off and it would hold the steam valve right in so that there was no leakage to waste steam. I remember an occasion when a hook came off.

'It was on the 3.30am goods out of Bath. We had No 53803. She'd just come back from the shops and she was lovely — beautiful riding, and it was only about the second trip since she'd come back. We had a full load. Norman Rosenburg was driving the banker at the back. We got going and just as we were emerging from Devonshire Tunnel the hook came off. The brake shot out. I spotted it straight away and pushed it in, but I wasn't quick enough, the wagons buffered into 53803. Norman felt this, thought I was stopping, and shut his regulator.

'In the meantime I just pushed the brake in, held it until I could turn the steam valve on and we continued. I took that train up through Lyncombe Vale to the head of the gradient on my own — Norman was stopped back there in the tunnel — but we managed it alright. I had to drop her nearly into full forward gear to get her over the top, but she made it.' (It would have been very dangerous for the banker to have tried to make contact again with the train. It might have been all right in daylight, but not at night or in a tunnel, for the banker may have struck the brake van too violently and caused a derailment.) 'Norman told me later that he listened to make sure that I made it. Norman also knew what had happened — he was no fool.'

4
Run down and closure

'It's curtains for us, I'm afraid,' said the signalman months before closure of the S&D was announced officially. He had almost wept when he last travelled up the line to which he had devoted a lifetime of service. He felt ashamed of the peeling paint on the stations reduced to unstaffed halts, their prize-winning gardens run wild, signal-boxes gutted and sidings ripped up.

He had watched the running-down process: the withdrawal of the 'Pines Express', the holiday trains and excursion traffic, the re-routeing of through freight, the creeping sense of dereliction and decay; the Swift & Delightful had become the Slow & Dirty.

While the storm clouds were beginning to gather and threaten the S&D, one very unusual event took place on 9 June 1961. The Bath Festival Committee always arranged an unusual dance, and that year it was held on Green Park station and attended by about 1,000 people. Humphrey Lyttleton was the star performer assisted by the Avon Cities and the Pearce Cadwallader jazz bands. A DMU took guests to a barbecue at Wellow, while in the waiting

Lamp Section

In rural Somerset and Dorset the lighting of station approaches and platforms was often primitive and barely adequate. Paraffin oil lamps in a variety of forms ancient and modern were being lit in the winter evenings of 1965 and 1966. The S&D, and later the Western and Southern Regions of BR did not consider the heavy cost of wiring and installing electric lighting worthwhile. At Highbridge gas lamps hissed on the S&D platforms.

Far left:
Oil lamp on standard at Binegar. Notice the decorative ventilator at the top. *C. Steane*

Left:
Wall-mounted oil lamp with a large shiny reflector. The front opens to give access so that the lamp can be taken out, cleaned and replenished with oil and the wick trimmed. *C. Steane*

Right:
Pressure lamp at Wellow.
C. Steane

Below:
Pressure lamp at Edington
Burtle. This pattern is suspended
and could be lowered on a
pulley. Note weight to assist
lowering when lamp unhooked.
C. Steane

room at Green Park, a non-stop showing was given of the film 'The Titfield Thunderbolt'.

Even as early as 1961 S&D closure was expected, Councillor W. D. Hartley representing Wellow on the Bathavon Rural Council said on 28 June that about 100 people from Wellow alone used the line daily, travelling to Bath, Radstock, or Midsomer Norton and that 'owing to the narrow and tortuous roads and to previous experience' a bus service would be an unsatisfactory alternative. On 17 October BR stated that it was not proposed to close the S&D in the near future. However, the October timetable, virtually unchanged since well before World War 2, made it impossible for a housewife from Norton or Radstock to travel into Bath for a morning's shopping and return in time to prepare lunch, and impossible to get into Bath for an afternoon's shopping unless she left home by 1.00pm. Furthermore, no convenient connections were provided to the north. To catch the 10.10am Bath to Mangotsfield which gave a connection to Birmingham, Sheffield and Newcastle, the S&D passenger had to kick his heels at Bath from 8.46am; while the Down stopping train which connected with the 'Pines' gave him more than an hour's wait at Bath when returning from the north. The line was certainly not making an all-out effort to get passengers to use it.

Although the excursion fares to Bournemouth and Burnham may have attracted travellers, one look at the timetable deterred them. Perhaps wisely the advertisements gave no idea of the ordeal which had to be undergone, especially on the return journey after a day at the sea. To travel to Bournemouth from Radstock one either had to leave at 7.18am and arrive at 10.45, (3½hr to travel 60 miles) or use the mid-morning train which arrived at 12.55, a little on the late side for lunch. Then there was the problem of returning. Your day at the seaside had to terminate before 3.40pm unless you were prepared to risk the 6.48pm all-stations to Templecombe where a 40min pause was allowed for recovery giving a 10.00pm arrival at Radstock.

A return from Burnham-on-Sea was similarly prolonged. You could leave at 4.00pm and tolerate a wait of 55min at Evercreech Junction, or alternatively leave Burnham at 7.10pm and arrive at Radstock 9.59pm, taking nearly 3hr for a distance of 30 miles as the crow flies, and allowing more than an hour to savour the amenities of Evercreech Junction. Although Sunday excursions to Bournemouth were well patronised, other resorts were rarely served by through trains. Weymouth, Lyme Regis,

Left:
Pressure lamps at Wellow lit and
ready to be hung. *C. Steane*

Seaton, Sidmouth, Budleigh Salterton and Exmouth were ignored, as was the revival of the prewar excursions to Clifton Down with the zoo admission charge included in the fare.

In 1961 it was still believed that the S&D could, and should be, made to pay, it certainly had potential since it served quite a few sizeable towns:

Bath	80,100
Norton/Radstock	12,320
Shepton Mallet	5,220
Wincanton	2,537
Sturminster Newton	1,800
Blandford	3,400
Broadstone	3,000
Poole	87,440
Bournemouth	143,500

The following year Howard Fry, prospective Liberal candidate for Wells, proposed running 40 or 65-seater diesel railcars at hourly intervals, these being cheaper to run than 120-seater steam trains, and faster than buses. Manning was to have been reduced by abolishing porters, ticket collectors, stationmasters and firemen, leaving just a driver and conductor-guard, the latter issuing tickets and dealing with parcels. BR management refused to give the suggestion a trial, yet 20 years later, this was to be standard practice on many BR stopping trains.

The beginning of the end for the S&D was the diversion of the 'Pines' on 8 September 1962, the last year the Friday night/Saturday morning trains ran during the summer holiday period. The WR claimed that

re-routeing the 'Pines' via Oxford and
Reading would give a very substantial saving
in train mileage. S. E. Raymond, General
Manager of the Western Region said that
the alterations were designed to improve the
service for 'the majority of our customers'
and to effect very necessary financial
economies. R. W. Croft in a letter to the
Bath *Evening Chronicle* wrote: 'Oxford and
Reading folk can get to Bournemouth by
rail, albeit by a somewhat circuitous route,
but in any case via London is a reasonable
proposition as far as they are concerned.

'Not so with Cheltenham, Gloucester and
Bath. Once the "Pines" has disappeared

then they are virtually denied access to
Bournemouth by rail. Ever tried going to
Bournemouth from Bath via the GW? You
won't attempt it again, once you have. Why
the abolition of the two Sunday excursions?
No prizes for guessing!

'I was informed by a Green Park official
— but I cannot vouch for accuracy –
that when the fare to Bournemouth was
10s on a Sunday, these two trains carried
1,400 passengers. A not unremunerative
proposition, I should think.'

The last 'Pines' over the S&D was
single-headed by Class 9F 2-10-0 No 92220
Evening Star. Although S&D enthusiasts

hoped against hope that this would not be a presage of the end of the line itself, deep in their hearts they knew that the end could not be far off.

The re-routed 'Pines' left Bournemouth West at 9.35am (10min earlier than when it travelled via Bath) and arrived at Manchester at 5.10pm (4.38pm via Bath) – an increased time of 42min. The mileage too was increased by 6½ from the 248¼ via Bath. Furthermore it failed to meet the Scottish connection at Crewe and involved Bournemouth passengers making a journey to Glasgow taking an additional 3hr. On its southward journey, the new timing of the 'Pines' was 16min longer than when it went via Bath. Furthermore, from the beginning of the winter timetable, not one southbound express of any importance called at Mangotsfield which meant that Bath Green Park and S&D stations were devoid of any connection from the north. No passengers to the north meant no tickets to the north and so S&D income was only from relatively low-price tickets issued for local journeys, with the result that the lower receipts 'proved' the line to be uneconomic. The final irony was the issue of a free booklet 'Improved Services between Bristol and the North' and as this publication included connections to and from Bath Green Park, a glance at it showed the absurdity of the 'Improved Services' title.

A severe blizzard at the end of 1962 caused problems. On Sunday 30 December, Driver Jack Stamp and Fireman Ken Gibbings were sent out on Class 3F 0-6-0T No 47557 to clear the tracks, as no trains had run that day and drifts had built up unhindered. The snow plough came to grief in a deep drift near Winsor Hill, and the engine ran out of water before it could be released, so its fire had to be dropped. The crew spent 8hr in a nearby permanent way hut until picked up by a rescue team sent out from Green Park on a Dorset '7'. Eventually the line was cleared and on 2 January 1963 trains were able to run between Bath and Evercreech Junction, double track being maintained as far south as Midsomer Norton, but from there, only a single line had been cleared to Evercreech Junction.

On 3 January more snow fell and re-blocked the line, trapping three trains. The night Mail train to Bournemouth left Bath with three engines, the first carrying a snow plough, but as they forced their way through a drift just south of Shepton Mallet, snow cascaded down into the cab and they became stuck in a 10ft deep drift. The crews started digging the engines out. To refresh themselves they brewed tea by melting down snow to get water, and dried their wet clothes in the cab. After 5hr they got the train moving again only to come up against further drifts. Freeing the engines a second time, they ran them light to Evercreech Junction to refill the water tanks which were running dry. Returning to their train, they found it buried under snow. The crew went back to Evercreech Junction where they were given a meal and offered accommodation. They declined the latter and decided to return to Bath by getting a taxi to Castle

Lineside Notices

Some plates were cast by the S&DJR at its Highbridge Works, while others were provided by the L&SWR or SR from stock.

Below:
An array of notices at Evercreech New. The left one is on a concrete pillar, those on the right attached to a post made from an old rail. *C. Steane*

Above:
A selection of cast iron plates at Evercreech New. *C. Steane*

Right:
S&D 'Trespassing on the Railway' sign dated 5 August 1903. *C. Steane*

Cary where they boarded a train from Weymouth, reaching Bath Spa 20hr after they had left Green Park. On 7 January the line was cleared and open through to Bournemouth, but only a single line was available between Binegar and Evercreech Junction. Shoscombe and Wellow were cut off by road drifts for many days, the only access being by rail, and villagers being impressed by the importance of the railway on their lives.

The appointment of Dr Richard Beeching as Chairman of the British Railways Board, followed by his 1963 plan for modernising rail services and cutting out little-used uneconomic lines, did nothing to reassure S&D supporters. Commenting on the Beeching Plan, Councillor W. G. Bartlett, chairman of Norton-Radstock Urban Council, voiced what many others believed, 'I should have thought that before the service was withdrawn completely a diesel service could have been tried with the driver issuing tickets. If they could run the trains at times convenient to the public it would also help.'

At a meeting on 22 May 1963 over 20 S&D stationmasters were told that their line was to close on 30 September and that 500 railwaymen would lose their jobs. This meeting was a 'preliminary and private discussion between management and staff into details of closure following the Beeching report', management being represented by H. E. Bastin, District Superintendent of the Bristol Division. An official announcement that the S&D was to close on 30 September was made on 12 June, but so many objections flooded in that the South Western Area Transport Users' Consultative Committee could not deal with them by the set deadline. Shoscombe was particularly angry at closure as, because of hills and narrow lanes, no buses could serve the area and many people were solely dependent on rail to take them to the outside world. Trains carried patients to doctors' surgeries in the Norton/Radstock area and to hospitals at Bath, while workers and shoppers depended on rail for their transport. The severe winter of 1962-63 was still very fresh in their minds when the railway was the only means of conveying milk and bread supplies to their isolated village.

On 10 January 1964 the South Western Area report cited cases of hardship if passenger services were withdrawn without bus services being improved. Those particularly affected were children living between Cole and Templecombe attending schools in Cole and Bruton; adults living in or near Bruton and Wincanton who would have been denied a rail service to and from Sherborne and Yeovil for work, shopping and hospital visiting; while residents of Street and Glastonbury would have lost a service to Bristol, Bath and other places. The committee suggested that a new bus service would alleviate these problems except for those living in the hilly country at or near Shoscombe.

On 7 September 1964 the night freight train and the 2.40am Bath to Bournemouth Mail were withdrawn, the line closing at night for the first time since the 1870s. Between 1963 and 1965 freight facilities were withdrawn from most intermediate stations and Midford, Wellow and Chilcompton reduced to unstaffed halts.

In June 1965 the expected bombshell came at last. It was announced that closure of the S&D would be in September. This date was later cancelled due to objections

Below:
Gradient post near Corfe Mullen. Such signs were very necessary for working loose-coupled freight trains so that a guard or fireman knew when to screw down, or release the brake in order that the train could be kept under control. *C. Steane*

Right:
Bus service Bournemouth Central to Bournemouth West after the 'temporary' closure of Bournemouth West.

Closure of Bournemouth West Station

Bus service between Bournemouth Central and Bournemouth West
6 September to 3 October 1965

MONDAYS TO SATURDAYS

DOWN Train due	Connecting bus departs Bournemouth Central	Connecting bus arrives Bournemouth West	UP Connecting bus departs Bournemouth West	Connecting bus arrives Bournemouth Central	Train departs
08 32	08 37	08 52	06 37 SX	06 52 SX	07 02 SX
10 45 SX	10 50 SX	11 05 SX	06 59	07 14	07 24
11 29	11 34	11 49	07 12	07 27	07 37
12 36	12 41	12 56	08 10	08 25	08 35
12 45	12 50	13 05	08 21	08 36	08 46
14 30	14 35	14 50	08 59	09 14	09 24
14 45	14 50	15 05	09 41	09 56	10 06
15 02 SO	15 07 SO	15 22 SO	10 03	10 18	10 28
15 27 SX	15 32 SX	15 47 SX	10 31	10 46	10 56
15 37 SO	15 42 SO	15 57 SO	10 42	10 57	11 07
16 28	16 33	16 48	12 09	12 24	12 34
16 43	16 48	17 03	12 34	12 49	12 59
17 59 SX	18 04 SX	18 19 SX	14 10	14 25	14 35
18 31 SX } 18 32 SO }	18 37	18 52	14 44	14 59	15 09
18 52	18 57	19 12	16 12	16 27	16 37
19 02 FO } 19 09 }	19 14	19 29	16 48	17 03	17 13
20 07 FO	20 12 FO	20 27 FO	18 10	18 25	18 35
20 28	20 33	20 48	18 26	18 41	18 51
20 44 FO	20 49 FO	21 04 FO			
20 52	20 57	21 12			
22 25 } 22 41 }	22 46	23 01			

FO—Fridays only. SO—Saturdays only. SX—Saturdays excepted.

SUNDAYS

DOWN			UP		
11 47	11 52	12 07	09 09	09 24	09 34
12 38	12 43	12 58	10 09	10 24	10 34
12 57	13 02	13 17	10 46	11 01	11 11
14 23	14 28	14 43	13 04	13 19	13 29
14 45	14 50	15 05	14 00	14 15	14 25
15 11	15 16	15 31	15 08	15 23	15 33
16 22	16 27	16 42	15 46	16 01	16 11
18 16	18 21	18 36	16 12	16 27	16 37
19 03½	19 09	19 24	17 10	17 25	17 35
19 19	19 28	19 43	17 47	18 02	18 12
21 39	21 44	21 59	18 29	18 44	18 54
22 03	22 08	22 23	19 11	19 26	19 36
23 34	23 39	23 54	20 03	20 18	20 28
			21 14	21 29	21 39

See overleaf for bus services between Branksome and Bournemouth West

Bus service between Branksome and Bournemouth West
6 September to 2 October 1965

MONDAYS TO SATURDAYS

DOWN Connecting bus departs Bournemouth West	Connecting bus arrives Branksome	Train departs	UP Train due	Connecting bus departs Branksome	Connecting bus arrives Bournemouth West
06 48 SX	06 58 SX	07 01 SX	08 06½	08 10	08 20
06 59 SO	07 09 SO	07 12 SO	09 00	09 03	09 13
09 31	09 41	09 44	10 42	10 45	10 55
11 35	11 45	11 48	13 05	13 08	13 18
13 07	13 17	13 20	13 51½	13 55	14 05
15 31 SX	15 41 SX	15 44 SX	18 09	18 12	18 22
15 37 SO	15 47 SO	15 50 SO	19 05	19 08	19 18
17 24	17 34	17 37			
18 40	18 50	18 53			

SO—Saturdays only. SX—Saturdays excepted.

British Rail | Southern Region

Published by British Railways, Southern Region AD 380/A4/27865

---

being received, a Transport Users' Consultative Committee meeting being held in October to consider these.

On 2 August the Bournemouth electrification scheme demanded the closure of Bournemouth West station and S&D trains were either terminated at Branksome, or diverted to Bournemouth Central on a so-called temporary basis, but they never returned to Bournemouth West, the Ministry of Transport agreeing to the station's closure on 4 October.

The announcement on 10 September 1965 that S&D passenger traffic was to be withdrawn on an unspecified date, coincided with the filming of R. L. Stevenson's comedy *The Wrong Box* at Green Park station.

Norman Down, stationmaster at Binegar and Ernie F. J. Cross signalman at the same station, called a mass meeting of railwaymen at Templecombe on 19 September. It was attended by 120 employees, two MPs, and four prospective candidates. The rail-

Right:
Shoscombe & Single Hill halt — in an area inaccessible by standard size buses. *C. Steane*

84

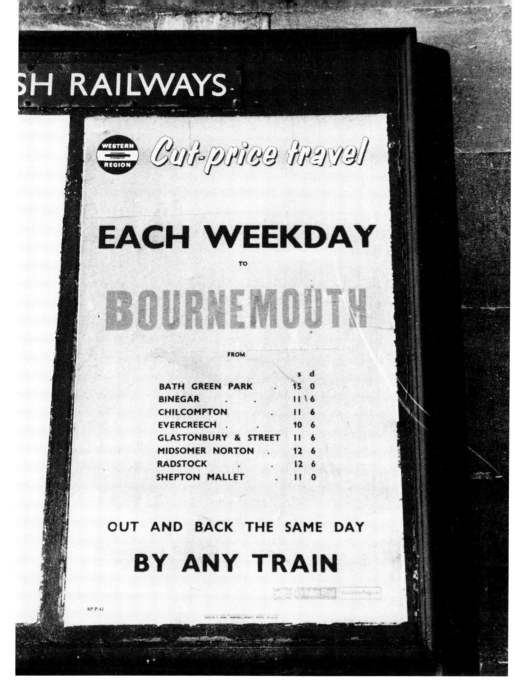

SH RAILWAYS

WESTERN REGION *Cut-price travel*

EACH WEEKDAY

TO

BOURNEMOUTH

FROM

		s	d
BATH GREEN PARK	.	15	0
BINEGAR	. .	11	6
CHILCOMPTON	.	11	6
EVERCREECH	. .	10	6
GLASTONBURY & STREET		11	6
MIDSOMER NORTON	.	12	6
RADSTOCK	. .	12	6
SHEPTON MALLET	.	11	0

OUT AND BACK THE SAME DAY

BY ANY TRAIN

RP/P/42

waymen accused the Western Region of 'cold-blooded, deliberate murder of the line, planned and carefully executed over a period of 10 years, way before Dr Beeching's plan'. They said that methods used by the authorities were the deliberate withdrawal of important through passenger trains, freight and parcel services, and the re-routeing of goods so that journeys took twice the time of the direct route and days instead of hours to reach their destination. The railwaymen also charged management with a refusal to modernise the line or its stations; to effect economies which railwaymen knew would work, but which 'college boy theorists' sitting at regional headquarters would not accept.

After referring to statements by the Transport Minister Tom Fraser and the Prime Minister Harold Wilson to the effect that no further major closures would be permitted pending completion of the national review of all forms of transport, the resolution sent to Mr Wilson stated: 'There is a widespread feeling by railwaymen, traders and the general public that a breach of faith has been committed in this case.'

Then, on 12 November 1965 an official announcement by a British Rail spokesman confirmed that all passenger services on the S&D were to be withdrawn on 3 January 1966 together with the majority of freight trains, but that withdrawal of the former was subject to alternative bus routes being provided to serve villages along the line. Mineral trains hauling coal from Writhling-ton Colliery near Radstock and milk tank wagons from dairies at Bason Bridge and Bailey Gate were to continue; while the line up to Blandford Forum from the south was to remain open for parcels and goods traffic. The nine passenger services each way daily

Western and Southern Regions   **British Railways Board**
Transport Act 1962

Withdrawal of railway passenger services

The Minister of Transport has given his consent to the Board's proposal to discontinue all passenger train services between **BRISTOL TEMPLE MEADS** and **BOURNEMOUTH WEST** and between **HIGHBRIDGE** and **EVERCREECH JUNCTION** and from the following stations and halts:—

FISHPONDS	CHILCOMPTON	SHILLINGTONE
STAPLE HILL	BINEGAR	BLANDFORD FORUM
MANGOTSFIELD	MASBURY HALT	BAILEY GATE
WARMLEY	SHEPTON MALLET	BROADSTONE
OLDLAND COMMON HALT	(CHARLTON ROAD)	CREEKMOOR HALT
	EVERCREECH NEW	BASON BRIDGE
BITTON	EVERCREECH JUNCT.	EDINGTON BURTLE
BATH GREEN PARK	COLE	SHAPWICK HALT
MIDFORD HALT	WINCANTON	ASHCOTT
WELLOW HALT	HENSTRIDGE	GLASTONBURY & STREET
SHOSCOMBE & SINGLE HILL HALT	STALBRIDGE	WEST PENNARD
RADSTOCK NORTH	STURMINSTER NEWTON	PYLLE HALT
MIDSOMER NORTON SOUTH		

The terms of the Minister's consent can be inspected at local booking/enquiry offices.

POSTPONED

... on ... 1966

Western and Southern Regions   **British Railways Board**
Transport Act 1962

Withdrawal of railway passenger services

BRISTOL — BATH (Green Park) — BOURNEMOUTH
and
HIGHBRIDGE — EVERCREECH JCN.

Passenger services will be withdrawn from the above sections of line on and from
MONDAY 7th MARCH, 1966

Closing

Above:
Posters announcing the withdrawal of passenger services were displayed on station boards in December 1965. Early in January 1966 they were amended as the closure had been postponed. *C. Steane*

Above right:
Poster announcing closure. *C. Steane*

between Bath Green Park and Evercreech Junction, the six Down and four Up through or connecting services between Bath and Bristol via Mangotsfield and the six Up and five Down trains between Evercreech Junction and Highbridge were to be discontinued.

A Western Region spokesman commented on this news: 'I don't think there is any reason to doubt that the bus services will be available. About 400 railwaymen are affected by the closures and a fairly large number will be declared redundant. The staff will be given every possible consideration. Each worker will be seen individually

and in a number of cases they will be offered alternative employment within the industry. In other cases arrangements will be made for a worker's resettlement when he will receive a generous allowance.'

However, a month later on 14 December, BR announced that the closure proposed on 3 January had been postponed. Wake's Services Ltd of Sparkford and Wincanton had proposed running a bus service between Blandford Forum, Glastonbury and Midsomer Norton and was to have laid this plan before the Western Traffic Commissioners for their approval. But the Managing Director was forced to withdraw the application due to a shortage of staff, coupled with too little time to organise the service adequately. As the Minister of Transport, Tom Fraser, had insisted that an alternative bus service must be provided before closure, the S&D was perforce, temporarily reprieved. The Traffic Commissioners' representative commented that they would now have to wait for a further application by a bus company. He anticipated that BR officials would call the operators together and that they would then forward a new application in the normal way for running the service required by the Minister.

One writer to the Bath *Evening Chronicle* implied that the reasons given by Wake's Services Ltd were not the whole truth. Mrs Anne Watts of Wellow, a village whose transport facilities were gravely threatened by the announced rail closure, wrote on 17 December, 'There is much rejoicing all along the S&D line at the news of its temporary reprieve, but I am most intrigued by the reasons given for the withdrawal of the application by the bus company. Our line has been under threat of closure for

Signals

about two years – ample time to organise staff and plans for a substitute bus service. Can it be that no bus company can be found which is willing to operate a service that will be unremunerative at the best of times and impossible to run with any regularity in bad winter conditions?

'Is it wishful thinking to hope that if all the bus companies turn down this job the Minister of Transport may at last see the point that we have been trying to make all these months?'

Two days before Christmas, BR announced an 'interim emergency service', of which one S&D railwayman commented

'It does not represent a service at all'. In the New Year four trains were to run daily each way from Bath to Templecombe and only one through to and from Bath to Bournemouth. The solitary through Up train left Bournemouth at 18.46 and arrived at Bath at 21.50 giving Bournemouth people no chance to return home that day. Someone from Bournemouth wishing to visit Bath would have had to leave at 09.37, arrive Templecombe 11.03 and kick his heels there until 14.00 when a train left for Bath, arriving there at 15.40 – 6hr to travel 73 miles. The passenger could then enjoy the Queen City of the West until 18.46.

BRITISH RAILWAYS - WESTERN REGION.

SOMERSET & DORSET LINE.

ADDITIONAL SERVICES.

EACH WEEKDAY ON AND FROM MONDAY 17 JANUARY, 1966.

UNTIL THE CLOSURE OF THE LINE.

Evercreech Junction	Dep.	17.02
Wincanton	Dep.	17.12
Templecombe	Arr.	17.20
Templecombe	Dep.	17.35
Wincanton	Dep.	17.43
Cole	Dep.	17.52
Evercreech Junction	Dep.	18.00
Pylle Halt	Dep.	18.04
West Pennard	Dep.	18.12
Glastonbury & Street	Dep.	18.23
Ashcott	Dep.	18.31
Shapwick Halt	Dep.	18.36
Edington Burtle	Dep.	18.42
Bason Bridge	Dep.	18.50
Highbridge	Arr.	18.59

THE 17.15 from Evercreech Junction to Highbridge will cease to run

Between 08.15 and 16.25 no S&D train left Green Park.

Publication of this new timetable provoked quick reactions from R. W. Gibson, County Councillor for Shepton Mallet who worked at Green Park station. Councillor Gibson told an *Evening Chronicle* reporter: 'At least 50% of the alternative bus services which were laid down as a minimum requirement before closure are not met by the new [rail] services.' From Binegar came a letter of cynical protest from Ivor Kenna, 'After a prolonged campaign of high fares, irregular services and downright discouragement or sabotage of freight – the best paying services, British Railways managed to render the S&D line unprofitable and to get permission for closure. Now that closure on 3 January has fallen through, due to lack of alternative bus services, British Rail are cutting down on services to such an extent as to make it unlikely that anyone will, or can use the line at all! Perhaps they reason that if nobody travels, no alternative buses will be needed. No ordinary firm works in this manner. Some deeper game is being played.'

Two days later the Somerset County Council entered the arena. In a telegram to the Minister of Transport now, after a Government reshuffle, Mrs Barbara Castle, the Council deplored 'the precipitant actions of the Railways Board regarding curtailment of the services on the S&D line in violation of the principles under the closure consent

Above:
Typed handbill announcing additional services from 17 January 1966.

Right:
A 'wrong road' or 'backing' signal at Midford. It enabled a train to be signalled from the single line on to the Up road. It was used, when for example, an Up goods stalled on the gradient and wished to return to the double track at Midford in order to raise more steam, or wait for a pilot. The lattice post is made from two rails. An old rail also formed the lamp post.
C. Steane

Far right:
Upper quadrant Up signal, Shillingstone. *C. Steane*

accepted by the Minister for public transport in the areas served'. It went on to urge that the Minister 'should intervene to prevent the curtailment of railway services before final closure'. This was a ponderous but emphatic protest and it received the support of the Norton-Radstock Urban Council and Bath-avon Rural Council which also appealed to the Minister.

Meanwhile the GPO authorities in North Somerset were calmly preparing for what seemed to them to be the inevitable: they announced their own road service for mail between Bath, Radstock, Shepton Mallet, Wells and Glastonbury, much of this having previously been carried under contract by the railway.

On 31 December the Somerset County Council explained that the only effect of its protest was that the Minister had asked the Railways Board to see what could be done to avoid hardship for regular S&D com-muters. On the same day a WR spokesman at Bristol was emphatic that nothing could be done outside the proposed emergency service; that there could be no extra buses or rail services in spite of the local authorities' complaints.

Meanwhile five special trains had been arranged to travel over the S&D to mark its closure at the first weekend in January 1966, but following the line's temporary reprieve, three were cancelled. The Locomotive Club of Great Britain ran one on 1 January 1966. The train hauled by BR Standard Class 9F 2-10-0 No 92243 failed on the Mangotsfield to Bath line at Warmley with a collapsed brick arch in its firebox had arrived at Bath 90min late. This was a portent of things to come on the S&D itself. Its driver admitted to a reporter: 'I won't really be sorry to see these engines go. You see, nobody cares about them any more, not enough to look after them and maintain them in proper working order anyway.' Signalman Ernie Cross stopped this special at Binegar and distributed leaflets protesting at the line's closure. Norman Down, the stationmaster, prepared a report on the incident to be sent by the next available train, but as none ran between 08.08 and 14.58, the report arrived late. Management not wishing to have its dirty linen washed in public, wisely over-looked the event.

On 6 January, two days after the emerg-ency service had started, the Public Health

Above:
Starter signals, Highbridge,
24 June 1961. Shunting bell near
foot of signal post on left enables
a shunter to communicate by
bell code with the Highbridge
East signalman to inform him of
intended movements.
Locomotive ex-GWR 0-6-0
No 3216. *R. E. Toop*

Right:
Midford Up outer home and
calling-on arm, 15 August 1959.
Footplatemen can speak to
signalman using the telephone
in the box at the foot of the
post. *Colin G. Maggs*

& Highways Committee of the Bathavon
Rural Council was told that 'a wholly
unsatisfactory reply' had been given by
British Rail to a telegram of protest sent by
them on 29 December. 'We objected to the
high-handed action and total disregard by
BR of the conditions imposed and to be
complied with before closure, namely the
institution of adequate and alternative bus
services. To many the curtailed service
amounts to closure with no alternative road
services, and as an absolute minimum, I am
to press that the curtailed services be
supplemented.'

Feelings were strong, not only in Council
Chambers but also in villages, public bars,
drawing rooms and kitchens. From 'Sans
Despair' of Wellow came a strong letter of
protest on 6 January: 'As a daily traveller on
the S&D, I, along with many of my fellow
travellers from Shoscombe and Midford feel
that I must protest at the latest reduction of
services on this line. At the moment we have
an inadequate rail service with no alternative
bus service – with the exception of the
trifling once-weekly service to Wellow on
Saturdays.' The writer then went on to
criticise the timing of the early morning
trains in the Emergency Timetable, the lack
of one at midday from Bath, and that there
was no late evening train – 'the 9.25pm from
Bath is too early for cinema and theatre
goers'. He went on to plead for a reasonable

Left:
Rare signal having an arm facing each way. It protects the siding to Clandown Colliery, Radstock, 14 August 1959. *Colin G. Maggs*

rail service: 'We know that we cannot expect frequent services, but is it too much to ask for transport to meet the needs of those who work in town as I do, shoppers and those requiring recreation and entertainment – a quick, cheap service to Bath at reasonable times, a service which because of the state of the roads, the increasing traffic, wintry conditions, and length of route the bus services cannot provide?'

All these telegrams and letters, and doubtless quick discussion over telephones and diplomatic action behind the scenes, resulted in three official announcements being made on 13 January. Firstly Paul Dean, Conservative MP for North Somerset released the text of a letter from Mr Swingler, Joint Parliamentary Secretary to the Minister of Transport: 'The Railways Board now appreciates that the new rail service

Goods & Parcels

Above right:
Porters' trucks and barrows at Blandford Forum. Notice that the one nearest the camera has the foot of its legs strengthened with cast iron and the wheel has a cart-type iron tyre. *C. Steane*

Right:
Two- and one-wheel porters' trucks at Edington Burtle.
C. Steane

leaves some gaps which the full alternative bus service will cover, and which might affect some users seriously. They have been urgently considering these difficulties, and will, if they cannot meet essential needs by any further train adjustment, discuss with the principal bus operators how any such gaps could be covered in the interim period. I am sure the Traffic Commissioners will consider sympathetically any emergency application for short-term licences for the period until they consider the applications for substantive licences for the full rail replacement services.'

The second announcement came from a British Rail spokesman. Released to the Press the statement read, 'To help in cases of hardship, we are arranging to augment train and bus services until the S&D line closes. Starting next Monday, an emergency bus service will run from Shoscombe to Bath. It will leave the Barn, White Hill, at 1.00pm, call at Wellow station at 1.12pm, and will arrive at Bath Green Park station at 1.37pm, returning immediately. In addition on Fridays and Saturdays, a bus will leave

Above:
BR tractor and trailers in yard at Blandford Forum 1966, this type of vehicle being articulated is easily manoeuvrable in confined spaces. Trailers can be left to be loaded or unloaded while the tractor is elsewhere. The yard is paved to rail surface to ease movement of road vehicles. Note the early type of BR arrow symbol. *C. Steane*

Left:
Interior of goods shed at Blandford Forum. It appears as if the platform has been raised in height at some period. Great variety of parcels prevents bulk handling. Lock-up shed or office in corner. Sliding doors on right give access to road vehicles. *C. Steane*

BRITISH RAILWAYS
WESTERN AND SOUTHERN REGIONS

SOMERSET AND DORSET LINE

REVISION OF PASSENGER TRAIN SERVICES FROM

3rd JANUARY 1966
UNTIL FURTHER NOTICE

Owing to one of the road operators withdrawing his application for a licence to provide some of the alternative road services forming part of the consent conditions laid down by the Minister of Transport and the consequent postponement of the Licensing Court, it has become necessary to defer the date of closure of this line.

A new closing date has yet to be announced, but as from 3rd January, 1966, all existing passenger services between the following places will be suspended. An interim emergency service will be introduced, full details of which are contained in this pamphlet.

The sections of line concerned are:

Bristol (T.M.) to Bath Green Park

Bath Green Park to Bournemouth

Highbridge to Evercreech Junction

December 1965   *Paddington and Waterloo*

Printed by J. W. Arrowsmith Ltd., Bristol

Above:
Handbill giving revised timetable
3 January 1966.

Above right:
Crane in West Pennard goods
shed. *C. Steane*

Right:
Children enjoy the wooden crane
in the otherwise empty goods
shed at Midsomer Norton in the
early spring of 1966. *C. Steane*

94

Shoscombe at 10.30am to allow housewives to do their weekend shopping at Bath.

'The 5.00pm train from Highbridge to Evercreech Junction will now be extended to Templecombe where it will arrive at 5.20pm, and the 5.15pm from Evercreech Junction to Highbridge will cease to run. It will be replaced by a train leaving Templecombe at 5.35pm, arriving at Evercreech Junction at 6.00pm and Highbridge at 6.55pm.'

Finally, the third announcement came from the South West Transport Users' Consultative Committee. Its statement read,

'We have been considering the many complaints regarding the inadequacy of the service introduced by British Rail on the line since 3 January. The committee fully appreciates the difficulties experienced by the Railways Board which prevented the closure of the line on that date, but felt that where serious hardships were now arising at Shoscombe, Wellow, Wincanton and Templecombe, certain steps should be taken to obviate or reduce them, pending the full implementation of the Minister's consent. The committee is pleased to report that the Board will be introducing certain emergency

Signalboxes

There were tall boxes, on or adjacent to platforms, where the signalmen were high above the line to view approaching rail and road traffic as at Blandford Forum and Evercreech Junction South. There were middle-sized boxes standing prominently at strategic junctions and crossings on the line as at Bath Junction, Radstock North and Corfe Mullen. There were many small boxes standing alone by the lineside on the Somerset levels as at Shapwick or at the end of a high viaduct as at Midford where single line tablets were handed out or taken in. There were a few derelict boxes as between the tracks at Winsor Hill on Mendip. From many boxes signalmen controlled opening and closing gates either by wheel or on foot.

Some boxes were timber framed and boarded throughout; others had stone or brick bases and timber frames for windows. Roofs were Welsh slates or Bridgwater tiles. All had a small coal fire and flue and were safeguarded by a line of fire buckets.

Right:
Evercreech Junction South signalbox. After closure, the adjacent pub was renamed 'The Silent Whistle'. *C. Steane*

measures to operate until the complete withdrawal of the rail services is effected, and when all the alternative road facilities are assured.'

Thus public opinion coupled with pressure by local government authorities had achieved a small victory. But what were these 'difficulties' experienced by the Railways Board? The large increase in the number of cars since 1945; the greater flexibility and economy of country bus services; the deliberate re-routeing of passengers and freight such as the 'Pines Express' via Oxford and Burton beer via Bristol; all these developments helped to make the line redundant. So, with its impending closure, both engines and rolling stock had been allowed to deteriorate. Steam engines were not maintained in first-class order and as lines in the Southern and Western Regions changed to electric traction or diesel haulage, so their steam

Above:
The LMS-type Bath Junction box. View towards Green Park with line from Mangotsfield on the far side. *C. Steane*

Below:
The timber-built box at Radstock North, view towards Bath with the notorious level crossing in the foreground. *C. Steane*

Right:
Shapwick signalbox on the Somerset Levels. Notice the board carrying mirrors so the signalman can check that no traffic is approaching before he closes the gates.   *C. Steane*

Below:
Corfe Mullen box, view towards Poole. Built of brick, its corners are rounded. Tablet catcher near foot of stairs. The double track becomes single beyond the gates. 25mph speed limit sign on left and behind it is the apparatus for delivering a tablet.   *C. Steane*

locomotives were moved to depots at Bournemouth, Templecombe and Bath for use on the S&D. When an engine failed it was not repaired, but remained idle until sent for scrap.

The railway authorities were certainly under strong fire from the travelling public. With the impending closure they had found it inadvisable to spend money on improvements, renovations and maintenance beyond the necessary minimum for safety. Engines and coaches were often in a filthy state and while the scenery over the Mendips remained as magnificent as ever, it was not easy to enjoy. Grime accumulated on windows as carriage cleaners were hard to find; maintenance staff were not recruited or replaced and it often became difficult to obtain spare parts for repairs. Steam leaked from many joints.

To work the special service from Shoscombe and Wellow, BR hired a minibus from Messrs J. Chivers, the operators of Somervale Coaches Ltd, Welton, Midsomer Norton, the same bus which was to be used on the feeder service from these villages to Peasedown after the final closure of the line. Unfortunately this service ran into difficulties on 17 January 1966, its very first day, because railwaymen declared it a 'pirate' operation. Three passengers used it from Bath to Shoscombe and two on the first return journey. No one paid, as staff refused to issue and collect tickets. The 14 men at Green Park who decided on this action issued the statement: 'Railwaymen employed at Bath Green Park station said today they will refuse to issue or collect tickets for passengers using the proposed private bus service to run from Shoscombe and Wellow to Green Park station. They are satisfied a rail service can be operated with the manpower and stock available at this station. In the circumstances we feel that hiring a bus service is a grave misuse of public money. We anticipate that a large number of residents in the Shoscombe and Wellow areas will refuse to use what is now regarded as a pirate bus service. We would also call attention of railway management to the fact that these proposed changes have been introduced without consultation with the staff representatives of the unions concerned.'

The Bristol District Council of the NUR also strongly condemned the bus service. The next day it put forward a positive suggestion that a train should leave Templecombe at 12.00 and arrive in Bath at 13.08, while on Fridays and Saturdays another should leave Templecombe at 09.05 and arrive Bath 10.46, departing for Templecombe at 13.10. It believed that it was possible to organise such a service with the existing stock and personnel. Meanwhile BR officials were meeting representatives of the

Below:
The stone, brick and timber-built box on the Up platform at Binegar. *C. Steane*

Right:
Interior of Binegar box.
C. Steane

Below right:
Interior of the box at Midford
with Tyer's No 6 Tablet
Apparatus on the far left.
C. Steane

Facing page:
The other end of the Midford
frame.   C. Steane

14 men at Green Park in an attempt to reach agreement in a truly Gilbertian situation. The talks carried on into the afternoon — and only one person used the midday bus from Shoscombe. On the third day BR promised that 'consideration would be given to the proposals made by the railwaymen' — and for the time being the 14 staff at Green Park were to work as normal. The minibus ran as planned, and no further alterations were made to the rail service.

Later that week another incident showed up the deterioration of locomotives and the increasing inefficiency of the operating procedure. It was considered so serious that on 24 January three stationmasters went to the Divisional Headquarters at Bristol Temple Meads to complain about conditions of the S&D, pressing for action to improve the maintenance of locomotives and rolling stock and complaining of increasing inconvenience to passengers caused by break-

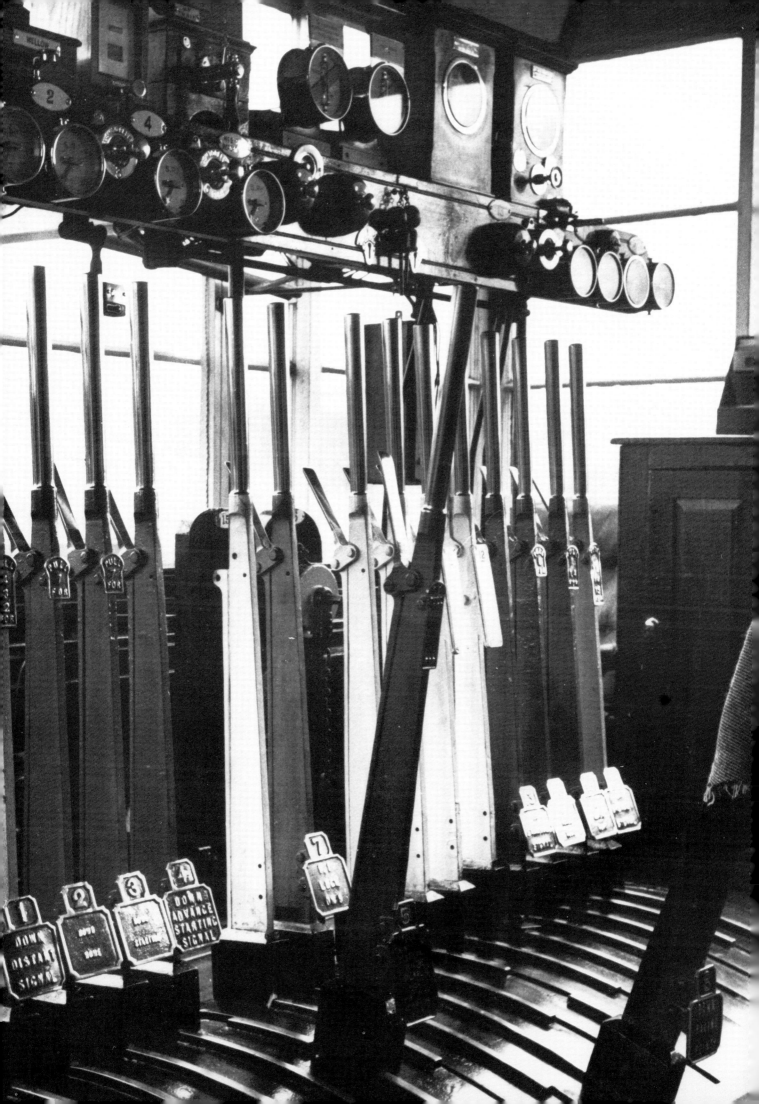

downs. The mounting criticism was brought to a head by two incidents. On 22 January the 07.00 from Templecombe due at Bath 08.50 arrived 2½hr late through the engine breaking down at Binegar. There the trouble had been compounded because railwaymen were unable to telephone direct to Central Control at Bristol and instead messages had to be passed down the line from signalbox to signalbox. This resulted in two engines being sent out to replace that which had failed, one being despatched from Bath and another from Shepton Mallet. Meanwhile passengers at Shoscombe and Wellow waited over two hours for the train to arrive. Railwaymen told the *Evening Chronicle* reporter: 'It is simply the result of bad maintenance. None of the engines on the line is in proper condition. They have been allowed to run down, and there is not the maintenance staff left to deal with the problems. Many have left because they expected to become redundant in a short while.'

Two days later the same train arrived over 20min late due to yet another engine failure. On both occasions the locomotive, originally with a rake of three coaches, had to leave two behind at Shepton Mallet because it had only sufficient power to pull one. 'This resulted', commented the *Evening Chronicle*, 'in passengers being crowded into the compartments of one coach' — but it did not reveal the number of people involved.

Divisional Headquarters gave assurance concerning the principal complaint regarding the difficulty of contracting Central Control. Until about two months before, signalboxes along the line were able to call Control direct by telephone, but then this facility was disconnected. In its place signalmen had to contact Control via Templecombe, but they found that this line was not always available. One railwayman said: 'Our concern is this is not so much over the poor running of the trains, but over what might happen in an emergency, a derailment, subsidence, accident or breakdown. It is often helpful, too, for a signalman to be able to obtain prompt guidance and advice from Control.' The stationmasters were assured that a direct link would be restored within a day or two.

On 26 January, BR made it clear that all their attempts to encourage Bournemouth

visitors to use the S&D services had proved fruitless. Almost vindictively it seemed, it announced that the cheap day return fare from Bath to Bournemouth was to rise from 15s 0d (75p) to 39s 0d (£1.95) — a rise of 160%. Other local fares were also increased, yet the posters advertising the former cheap rates remained on the hoardings, rain-soaked and begrimed, an ironic reminder of happier and more optimistic days on the S&D.

This increase in fares provoked more correspondence to the *Evening Chronicle*. On 19 January a letter writer commented bitterly: 'If any further proof was needed of the deliberate intention of British Rail to throttle the S&D, the announcement of a 160 per cent increase in the Bath to Bournemouth fare should provide it. Day return fares generally have been put up, but on the Great Way Round these have been kept down to a maximum of 20 per cent, yet on the S&D increases of 60 to 160 per cent are recorded.

'From Bath to London, 107 miles costs 37s 0d

'From Bath to Bournemouth, 72 miles costs 39s 0d!

'Yes! But of course one is by "God's Wonderful Railway" and the other is by "Sabotaged and Devastated".'

Other correspondents equally concerned about the fate of the railway made suggestions that it should be taken over by a private company. One pointed out the great difficulties: that the line was too long for a private company to run; the amount of capital required for necessary repairs would have been astronomical and that there could be no efficient service before these were carried out. Furthermore, recruiting staff to run such a company would certainly be difficult because without strong financial backing, jobs offered could have been only short term.

An efficient service would have proved hard to operate, as stopping trains would have duplicated the proposed new bus services making economic competition impossible. A more attractive proposition was the idea of running a fast service between Bristol and Bournemouth connecting the six main centres and working with co-ordinated bus services to and from the villages, but the need to operate trains over BR lines between Bournemouth and Blandford, Bristol and Bath made this almost a non-starter as BR held the ultimate weapon of non-co-operation.

There was a genuine concern too, whether the narrow lanes, many of them winding and steep, could carry extra traffic caused by the railway's closure. During January, Bathavon District Council wrote letters to the Ministry of Transport and the Economic Planning Council for the South West Region urging them 'to have the railway utilised to relieve the heavy traffic on the inadequate roads in the West Country. British Rail should investigate the possibility of operating a regular and reliable rail service for freight on the Somerset & Dorset line'.

C. H. Couchman of Wellow voiced the doubts of villagers when he wrote: 'Can the lanes from Wellow and Shoscombe to Bath carry a bus service in safety? Snow and ice on the roads cut off villages until the surface is heavily gritted. But no matter what the state of the weather the trains still run.'

For a fortnight after 29 January there was no further correspondence and no headlines in the *Evening Chronicle* about the future of the S&D apart from the fact that Norton Hill Colliery, once putting a considerable volume of traffic on the S&D, had closed on 11 February. Then on Monday 14 February came the news, not unexpected: 'S and D line may now close on March 7th'. 'British Rail are now planning to close the S and D railway, temporarily reprieved in January, on 7 March. This is subject to the Western Area Traffic Commissioners approving a number of applications now being heard by bus and coach operators to provide satisfactory alternative services. It is the biggest closure yet approved by the Government and will save more than £600,000 a year.'

That afternoon the Traffic Commissioners for the Western Area considered an application on behalf of Associated Motorways, Cheltenham, to run an express coach service between Bristol, Bath and Bournemouth. On Tuesday they heard applications by Somervale Coaches Ltd, to run the vital bus service between Blandford, Glastonbury and Midsomer Norton, linking the villages served by the S&D and also providing a local service between Shoscombe and Peasedown. Bath Tramways Motor Co applied to run a new service from Cole railway station to Bath. Somerset County Council and Bathavon Rural Council opposed these applications. Mr Hartley, a Wellow Parish Councillor, claimed that the proposed route was unsuitable for heavy public transport. He mentioned the narrow lanes from the Burnt House, Odd Down to Wellow; and from Hinton Charterhouse to Wellow and Peasedown, yet he was prepared to accept bus services as substitute for trains when these roads were widened. The Surveyor for the County Council had no objection to buses 'when the road improvements were completed'. Wake's Services also objected. Back in December it had withdrawn its application to provide an alternative service and so obtained a

temporary reprieve for the S&D but now opposed competitors stepping in as Somervale's proposed service from Blandford to Midsomer Norton via Glastonbury would have affected a service already licensed by Wake's. The Traffic Commissioners persuaded them to get together with Somervale Coaches and co-operate in running a service. Finally on Wednesday 16 February the Commissioners granted 13 applications for licences to provide the necessary bus and coach services:

1. Associated Motorways: Bristol and Bath to Bournemouth along the S&D route.
2. Bath Tramways Motor Co: Bath to Shortwood (north of Mangotsfield).
3. Bath Tramways Motor Co: Bath to Cole.
4. Bristol Omnibus Co: Wells to Highbridge.
5. Somervale Coaches: Shoscombe to Peasedown.
6. Somervale Coaches: Blandford Forum to Glastonbury and Midsomer Norton.
7. Western National: Glastonbury to Bruton.
8. Southern National: Yeovil to Gillingham.
9. Southern National: Yeovil to Sturminster Newton.
10. Southern National: Salisbury to Weymouth.
11. Wilts & Dorset Motor Services: Salisbury to Weymouth.
12. Bere Regis & District Motor Services: Woolland to Blandford Forum.
13. Hants & Dorset Motor Services: Stalbridge to Bournemouth.

The *Evening Chronicle* headlines that night were clear and definite: 'The S&D gives way to buses on March 7.'

At the end of the hearing the Chairman, Mr Samuel Gibbon KC, felt it necessary to give a word of explanation to the Press. He said that many people were under a misapprehension as to the power and function of the Commissioners. It was not their task or within their jurisdiction to decide in any way whether the S&D should continue. They had to decide on the assumption that if it closed, certain facilities would be needed. Their decision was based on the assurance that the bus and coach companies could implement their proposals with both vehicles and staff. 'If we found as a result of this that other vital services already licensed were being denuded or starved, and people were having to walk in Bath to provide services on the Mendips, then we should feel we have been misled.' In

BRITISH RAIL

Divisional Manager,
South Western Division.
19, Worple Road,
WIMBLEDON, S.W. 19.

Divisional Manager,
Bristol Division,
Transom House,
Victoria Street,
Bristol.

DETAILS OF ADDITIONAL AND/OR AMENDED OMNIBUS SERVICES WHICH
WILL BE AVAILABLE WHEN PASSENGER SERVICES ARE WITHDRAWN
FROM THE SOMERSET & DORSET LINE ON AND FROM
MONDAY 7TH MARCH, 1966.

Page.	Service Operated by:-	POINTS SERVED :-
1.	Bath Tramways	Bath;Warmley;Shortwood.
1 & 2.	Bath Tramways	Bath;Midford;Wellow;Shoscombe;Radstock; Midsomer Norton;Binegar;Masbury;Shepton Mallet;Evercreech;Bruton;Cole.
2.	Somervale Coaches	Shoscombe;Single Hill.
3.	Somervale Coaches	Glastonbury;West Pennard;Midsomer Norton; Chilcompton;Binegar;Shepton Mallet; Evercreech;Cole;Bruton;Wincanton;Gillingham; Henstridge;Stalbridge;Sturminster Newton; Shillingstone;Blandford Forum.
4	Western National	Glastonbury;West Pennard;Shepton Mallet.
4	Southern National.	Stalbridge;Sturminster Newton.
4	Train services	to and from Gillingham.
5	Southern National	Gillingham;Wincanton;Templecombe;Henstridge; Sherborne;Yeovil.
6	Toop & Ironside. (Bere Regis)	Sturminster Newton;Shillingstone;Blandford Forum.
6	Hants & Dorset	Stalbridge;Sturminster Newton;Shillingstone; Blandford;Broadstone;Poole.
7	Bristol Omnibus	Wells;Glastonbury;Ashcott;Shapwick;Edington; Burtle;Bason Bridge;Highbridge.
7	Assoc.Motorways	Throughout service Bristol - Bournemouth.

DO NOT CLIMB ABOVE FOOTPLATE LEVEL WHEN UNDER ELECTRIFIED WIRES

BATH GREEN PARK M.P. Depot   BRITISH RAILWAYS *WESTERN* Region   B.R. 32711/3

ENGINEMEN'S ROSTERS   Commencing *MONDAY 28·2·1966*

WEEK-ENDING 5TH MARCH 1966   S & D. SPECIALS

TRAINS	SUN	MON	TUE	WED	THUR	FRI	SAT	TRAINS	SUN	MON	TUE	WED	THUR	FRI	SAT
6·45	76026	76011	76005	76026	76005	76024		10·45 SPL							48766
8·15	80041	80036	80041	80038	80041	48760		11·0 Ass							34057
4/25	80041	80043	80043	41283	80043	80043		3·40 SPL							34057
6/10	80041	80038	80041	80038	80041			3/50 Ass							34006
S·X· 6·20	48760	48760	48760	48760	48760	✓									
5·25	3681	3681	47506	3681	3681	3681									
S·X· 1/50					✓										

MID DIVISION

S & D SPECIALS   SUNDAY 6TH MARCH

TRAINS	SUN	MON	TUE	WED	THUR	FRI	SAT	TRAINS	SUN	MON	TUE	WED	THUR	FRI	SAT
M·X· 3·15	✓	48309	48309	48309	48309	48309		10·30 Ass	48706	✓	✓	✓	✓	✓	✓
M·X· 4·40	✓	48706	48706	48706	48706	48706		10·30 SPL	80043	✓	✓	✓	✓	✓	✓
S·X· 1/0	48309	48309	48309	48309	48309	✓		SPARE	48760						
S·O· 3/25	✓	✓		✓	✓	✓									
S·X· 9/25	48760	48760	48760	48760	48760	✓		5/18 SPL		✓	✓	✓	✓	✓	✓
								5/10 Ass		✓	✓	✓	✓	✓	✓

the event these bus services proved no more viable financially than the railway they replaced and most were withdrawn after running only a few months.

No further correspondence appeared in the *Evening Chronicle*; either the Editor or the public had decided that there was no point in further protests about the demise of the S&D. On 5 March, Bath Tramways Motor Co inserted in the paper a formal notice: 'Following the closure of the Somerset and Dorset Railway the Bath Tramways Motor Co announce that Replacement Bus Services will be operated commencing Monday March 7 between Bath and intermediate points to Shepton Mallet and Cole.' All was ready for the takeover by road from rail.

On Saturday 5 March, the last day of scheduled services over the S&D, a booking clerk said to a prospective passenger intending to catch the last train out of Green Park, 'You'll be crushed to death. Hundreds have booked for the 18.10. They've come from all over to see us. Train enthusiasts from Sheffield and London have booked in for the night at Bath so that they can make this last journey.' He sold a record number of tickets for the 18.10 to Bournemouth, most passengers buying an 11s 0d (55p) return to Templecombe so that they could travel back on the final return service due in Bath at 21.58.

This last Up train was hauled by two Class 4MT 2-6-4Ts, No 80041 piloted by No 80043. At Evercreech Junction a scene

Above:
Locos scheduled to work regular and special trains over the S&D during the last weekend.

Left:
Duplicated booklet advising of alternative bus services after closing the S&D.

took place which showed a deep seriousness underlying the good fun and the giggle. A procession moved along the Down platform, crossed the lines to the Up and threaded its way through the dense crowd to the waiting train. There a local florist, dark-suited with a black coat and shining topper, halted the four men behind him — the stationmaster Mr Alexander Stowe and three of his uniformed staff all wearing mourning purple ribbons in their buttonholes. They carefully lowered a coffin surmounted by a cross of yellow flowers, into the guard's van. In the regrettable absence of a brass band, a loudspeaker relayed 'John Brown's Body' from a record player in the booking office. The black-edged card pinned to the wreath read: 'The Somerset and Dorset Railway died today, March 5 1966'. At the train's next stop, Evercreech New, the borrowed coffin was off-loaded into a hearse and the flowers went with the florist.

The train was so delayed at various stations that hundreds of spectators at Bath had to wait until 22.47 for it to appear. The *Evening Chronicle* recorded: 'People packed every compartment. Corridors took the overflow, making it quite impossible to move from one end of the coach to the other. But the majority didn't care. Detonators detonated, tape-recorders recorded, flashlights flashed and daffodils waited as the redundant "Pines Express" steamed in. "This is an unhappy moment," said one passenger as he alighted. "But I suppose it had to come," he added with a winsome smile.

'Why had he and others made this uncomfortable trip? Another passenger, Bryan Gibson, of Redland, Bristol, explained: "It's the romance of a passing beauty." How had he spent the journey? "Just sitting near the window, watching the stations go by and reminiscing," he said. David Hawkings, a civil servant from Kensington, added a last word, "For me this journey will be a reminder of the romance of the railway in its heyday. There's a decadent beauty about steam".'

The last day on which trains ran according to the timetable (or at least approximately!), ended with a mystery. At Evercreech Junction the North signalbox by the side of the Highbridge line was burnt down, only its stone base and some of the control equipment remaining. The box had been manned each day from 07.00 until 22.00; the coal fire in the small grate was never allowed to burn through the night. Was this final conflagration in the nature of a funeral pyre? Did the signalman prefer to see his tidy instruments and shining levers destroyed and blackened rather than fall into the hands of souvenir hunters, or go dusty and rusty through neglect? 'We don't know if this is arson or not,' said a policeman, 'there is very little left of the building to help investigators.' Did he really want to know?

The blaze which Shepton Mallet firemen spent some hours fighting made it necessary for special arrangements to be planned to allow the two Sunday special trains chartered by the Stephenson Locomotive Society and the Railway Correspondence & Travel Society to run through the junction.

Altogether, closure of the S&D put 350 staff out of work and the closure of 105 miles with its 36 stations and halts, four tunnels, 13 viaducts and 104 bridges was the longest stretch to go under Beeching.

Probably the place most seriously hit by the S&D's closure was Templecombe. This railway village with a population of just over 800 having about one in six of its inhabitants earning a living on the railway, some 130 being employed; the payroll after S&D closure being reduced to three signalmen each day working an eight-hour shift in the signalbox on the Waterloo to Exeter line.

On Monday morning, 7 March, the bus companies took on the job of carrying commuters, shoppers and other travellers to and from the villages and towns. But trains still ran on sections of the S&D. Blandford remained open for goods and parcels traffic; the dairies at Bailey Gate and Bason Bridge still sent away milk and cream by rail. Instead of a steam locomotive working out of Bath to collect coal from Writhlington Colliery, a diesel-hydraulic from Bristol travelled via Hallatrow to Radstock and over the newly constructed spur and up the S&D Down line to the pit. Its schedule was appropriately vague: 'Oh, it goes up just before two and comes back about a quarter to three.' Apart from these sections which remained in use, track and buildings surprisingly soon assumed a disused, derelict appearance. The running surface of the rails rusted within hours and signal arms, lamps and station nameboards fell into the hands of souvenir hunters. By May, grass had sprouted and weeds were flourishing on platforms.

The unclosed sections of the S&D did not last long:

Bath Junction-Bath Co-op siding closed 30 November 1967

Broadstone-Blandford Forum closed 6 January 1969

Highbridge-Bason Bridge closed 11 December 1972

Writhlington-Radstock closed 19 November 1973.

The Swift & Delightful had become the Sad & Derelict.

SLS trip Bath to Bournemouth, Sunday 6 March 1966

Above:
Class 8F 2-8-0 No 48706 and BR standard Class 4MT 2-6-4T No 80043 have climbed from the Bath shed to the main line preparatory to reversing on the coaches at Green Park station. The '8F' had worked coal trains from Writhlington in previous months and the '4MT' passenger trains. *C. Steane*

Left:
The train stands on one of the centre roads ready to leave. The red and white squares at the end of the bridge warn of limited clearance between track and outside of bridge. *C. Steane*

BRITISH RAILWAYS.

STEPHENSON LOCOMOTIVE SOCIETY (MIDLAND AREA).

Last Train over Somerset and Dorset Joint Line,
Sunday, 6th March, 1966.

	Arrive.	Pass.	Depart.	Note.
Bath Green Park			10.30	
Radstock North		10.49		
Shepton Mallet.	11.17		11.27	P
Evercreech Junction.	11.36		11.46	P
Wincanton		12.02		
Templecombe Upper.	12.10		12.25	P
Templecombe Junction	12.27		12.30	
Stalbridge		12.39		
Sturminster Newton.		12.49		
Blandford Forum		13.06		
Broadstone		13.23		
Poole	13.30		13.31	C
Bournemouth Central.	13.42		15.20	
Poole	15.30		15.31	C
Broadstone		15.38		
Blandford Forum		15.55		
Sturminster Newton		16.11		
Stalbridge		16.17		
Templecombe Junction	16.26		16.29	C
Wincanton		16.35		
Evercreech Junction	16.50		16.55	W
Shepton Mallet		17.06		
Radstock North		17.26		
Bath Green Park	17.44			

Notes: P - Photographic stop.
        C - Stop for trainmen only.
        W - Stop for water.

Power: 2 x 76 XXX Class Locos.

Passengers may retain their tour tickets as a souvenir of the journey.

Passengers from Birmingham, Cheltenham and Gloucester travel by connecting DMU. train in following times:-

dep	07.58	Birmingham New Street	arr	20.36
"	09.11	Cheltenham Spa Lansdown	"	19.38
"	09.24	Gloucester Eastgate	"	19.22
arr	10.15	Bath Green Park.	dep	18.25

PASSENGERS WILL BE PERMITTED TO TRAVEL BY THIS CONNECTING TRAIN ONLY ON PRODUCTION OF THIS NUMBERED ITINERARY AND THE VALID TOUR TICKET FROM BATH.

The Stephenson Locomotive Society announce that:-

1. Replacement tickets, properly dated, will be issued on the train in exchange for the ticket now issued.

2. D.M.U. Train from Birmingham.
   Cheltenham and Gloucester members entrain into the rear vehicle of the DMU. set on outward journey.

3. Reserved accommodation on special train from Bath will be as
    follows:-

    a. Bath Railway Society party travel in coaches 3 and 4
        from front.

    b. Bristol R.C.T.S. party travel in coach 5 from front.

    c. Cheltenham/Gloucester R.C.T.S. party travel in front
        half of coach 6 from front of train.

    d. Coach 7 from front of train will be reserved for
        parties of 4, 8 or multiples of 4 and members requiring
        such reservations should advise Mr.H.Brenholz,
        12, Chadbrook Crescent, Brook Road, Birmingham.15.
        A plan will be made available at Bath of these
        reservations.

4. A mile by mile itinerary, map of route, gradient profile
    and 16-page photographic brochure will be distributed on the
    train.   A limited number of copies of the HISTORY OF THE
    SOMERSET AND DORSET RAILWAY (Oakwood Press) will be on sale on
    the train at 10/6.

5. No refreshment facilities will be available on the train and
    thus an allowance has been made for extended stay at Bournemouth.

Below:
At Writhlington the Special was
halted, reversed to the Up line
and with a pilot aboard the
leading engine, travelled as far
as Midsomer Norton 'wrong
road'. The siding, left, leads to
the colliery. *C. Steane*

Right:
It travelled 'wrong road' because south of Radstock station a permanent way gang in the early hours that Sunday had already slewed the Down line and connected it with a spur from the ex-GWR's Bristol to Frome line. This link was made to enable Writhlington coal to be taken away after closure of most of the S&D. A permanent way train hauled by a 'Hymek' diesel-hydraulic stands in the distance on the former GWR branch.
C. Steane

Below:
Climbing the 1 in 50 gradient towards Masbury.   *C. Steane*

Above:
Descending past the derelict Winsor Hill signalbox, the only signal cabin on the Bath extension built of stone. The train is about to enter the original tunnel, 239yd in length. The Up line, right, emerges from the newer tunnel only 126yd long; in fact daylight can just be seen at the far end. On the right is a derelict siding of Hamwood Quarry closed c1940. *C. Steane*

Left:
Shepton Mallet, Charlton Road. The Special made a photographic stop on its way south. Illustrated here are the various building materials used by the S&D construction and maintenance men — local Lias and oolitic limestones, Welsh slates, cream-painted timber, red and blue bricks from Staffordshire, corrugated iron, steel posts and rails, Bridgwater tiles, iron castings perhaps originating from Highbridge Works, poles from Scandinavia, asphalt and — not visible — Pennant Grit paving stones.
C. Steane

Facing page, top:
Photographers gather at the lineside between Shepton Mallet and Evercreech Junction. *C. Steane*

Facing page, bottom:
Evercreech Junction North signalbox burnt to its stone base the previous night. The line from Highbridge comes in on the right. Note: inspection pit in foreground; lineman up telegraph pole near signalbox, and shunting signal. *C. Steane*

Above left:
No 48706 has its water topped up at Evercreech Junction. The siding between the Up and Down roads was used for stabling pilot engines waiting to assist heavy trains over the Mendips. The tracks were unusually far apart, a legacy of the broad gauge. *C. Steane*

Left:
An army of enthusiasts, many armed with cameras, stretch their legs at Evercreech Junction while the engines are taking water. *C. Steane*

Right:
Locomotives at Bournemouth depot, the centre one being BR Standard Class 5MT 4-6-0 No 73113 *Lyonnesse* with an unidentified Standard Class 4MT 2-6-0 beyond. There is a long pile of ash and clinker in the foreground. *C. Steane*

Centre right:
Passing Broadstone on the return journey. Speed limit 20mph. *C. Steane*

Bottom right:
The termination of Green Park as a passenger station. Locomotives are Nos 48706 and 80043. *C. Steane*

Facing page, top:
No 80043 in Cashmore's scrapyard, Newport, late spring 1966. *C. Steane*

Facing page, bottom:
Diesel-hydraulic No D7004 in the spring of 1966 coming off the S&D on to ex-Great Western metals at the newly-opened Radstock Junction. Radstock West ground frame can be seen in the left foreground. *C. Steane*

Dereliction & Destruction

Facing page:
A broken station window, 1967.
C. Steane

Left:
Evercreech New 1967. View Up
showing goods shed beyond the
passenger station. The break in
the platform wall on the left is
where signal wires and point
rodding emerged from the
signalbox before its closure,
11 October 1964. *C. Steane*

Below:
Green Park during track lifting.
C. Steane

Right:
Planet locomotive on demolition train on the Bridgwater branch just west of Edington Burtle. Ex-GWR bogie bolster 'C' for carrying rails. 29 August 1956. *Colin G. Maggs*

Below:
Scene of dereliction at Highbridge, summer 1966. *C. Steane*

Facing page, top:
Midsomer Norton, February 1967: view towards Radstock, former siding to Norton Hill colliery curving away to right. *C. Steane*

Facing page, bottom:
Broken door, Midsomer Norton, February 1967. *C. Steane*

Above:
Midsomer Norton, February 1967. Every pane in signalbox and greenhouse is smashed and glass scattered over the platform. Brambles and weeds grow along the embankment at this former prize-winning station.   *C. Steane*

Right:
The single platform halt at Henstridge is a sorry sight in June 1966. Vandals had smashed glass . . .   *C. Steane*

122

Left:
. . . pulled out drawers — but left untouched a fine set of bright brass handles on the booking office drawers. Fragments of glass are all over the floor.
C. Steane

Below:
At Lamyatt the crossing gates are damaged. View taken in June 1966. *C. Steane*

Right:
204bhp diesel-mechanical 0-6-0 No D2175 on track-lifting train near Pylle. Rails are lifted on to bogie wagon by the crane on the left. *C. Steane*

Below:
Pylle halt after track lifting. *C. Steane*

Facing page, top:
Wagons of lifted rails at Glastonbury. Tor beyond. Shunter seems perplexed. *C. Steane*

Facing page, bottom:
Starting in March 1967 the track was lifted north of Shillingstone. Rails and sleepers were taken over S&D metals through Templecombe to Radstock North where this train, headed by a diesel-hydraulic, stood waiting to be reversed over the new connecting spur to the North Somerset line en route to South Wales. *C. Steane*

5

Locomotive allocations

The lists shown here cover sheds on the ex-S&D system as at May 1959 and May 1965. Former S&D numbers are given in brackets after the BR number.

The left-hand column represents the 1959 allocation whilst the right-hand one is for 1965.

Bath, Green Park and sub-sheds at Radstock and Highbridge

GWR '57xx' class 0-6-0PT
3742	3681
	3758

GWR '94xx' class 0-6-0PT
	8436
	8486

LMS Class 2P 4-4-0
40601
40696
40697
40698
40700

LMS Class 2MT 2-6-2T
41241
41242
41243
41296
41304

LMS Class 3F 0-6-0
43682

LMS Class 4F 0-6-0
44096	44558 (58)
44146	
44422	
44523	

44558 (58)
44559 (59)
44560 (60)
44561 (61)

LMS/Sentinel 0-4-0TG
47190 (101)
47191 (102)

LMS Class 3F 0-6-0T
47275	47276
47316 (25)	47506
47465	47544
47496	
47557	

LMS Class 8F 2-8-0
48309
48444
48525
48660
48737

S&D Class 7F 2-8-0
53800 (80)
53801 (81)
53802 (82)
53803 (83)
53804 (84)

53805 (85)
53806 (86)
53807 (87)
53808 (88)
53809 (89)
53810 (90)

BR Class 5MT 4-6-0
73019	73001
73028	73051
73047	73054
73049	73068
73050	
73051	
73052	

BR Class 4MT 4-6-0
75071
75072
75073

BR Class 3MT 2-6-2T
82041	82004
	82041

Totals
1959 49 of which 18 were ex-S&D locomotives
1965 19 of which 1 was an ex-S&D locomotive

Templecombe

GWR '2251' class 0-6-0
3201
3205
3218

GWR '57xx' class 0-6-0PT
9651	4631

LMS Class 2P 4-4-0
40563
40564
40569
40634 (45)

LMS Class 2MT 2-6-2T
41248	41208
	41214
	41243
	41296

LMS Class 3F 0-6-0
43194 (62)
43216 (72)
43218 (73)
43248 (75)
43427
43436

LMS Class 4F 0-6-0
44102
44135
44417
44557 (57)

LMS Class 3F 0-6-0T
47542

BR Class 4MT 4-6-0
75072
75073

BR Class 4MT 2-6-4T
80043
80059
80067

BR Class 3MT 2-6-2T
82039

Totals
1959 18 of which 6 were ex-S&D locomotives
1965 13 of which none were ex-S&D locomotives